I Ask You,
Be Shepherds

I Ask You, Be Shepherds

— Reflections on Pastoral Ministry —

JORGE MARIO BERGOGLIO
POPE FRANCIS

Translated by
Michael O'Hearn

A Herder & Herder Book

THE POPE FRANCIS RESOURCE LIBRARY

The Crossroad Publishing Company
www.CrossroadPublishing.com

English translation copyright 2015
by The Crossroad Publishing Company
A Herder&Herder Book
The Crossroad Publishing Company, New York

The texts of *I Ask You, Be Shepherds* are taken from two sources:
(1) From *El verdadero poder es el servicio*, Editorial Claretiana,
Buenos Aires, Argentina. Chapter titles in the original Spanish
publication have been altered in this English edition with
the consent of Editorial Claretiana. These texts are exclusively
published by Crossroad in English. (2) Courtesy of
and with approval of the Libreria Editrice Vaticana.

The stylized crossed letter C logo is a registered trademark of
The Crossroad Publishing Company.

ISBN 978-0-8245-2057-1 (alk. paper)

Library of Congress Cataloging-in-Publication Data
available from the Library of Congress.

Cover design by George Foster
Book design by The HK Scriptorium, Inc.

In continuation of our 200-year tradition of independent publishing, The Crossroad
Publishing Company proudly offers a variety of books with strong, original voices
and diverse perspectives. The viewpoints expressed in our books are not necessarily
those of The Crossroad Publishing Company, any of its imprints or of its employees.
No claims are made or responsibility assumed for any health or other benefit.

Books published by The Crossroad Publishing Company may be purchased at
special quantity discount rates for classes and institutional use. For information,
please e-mail sales@CrossroadPublishing.com

Printed in the United States of America in 2015

Contents

Contents

Words from the Upper Room

IT IS A GREAT GIFT that the Lord has given us by bringing us together here in the Upper Room for the celebration of the Eucharist. I greet you with fraternal joy, and I wish to express to you my affection. I assure you of a special place in my heart and in my prayers. Here, where Jesus shared the Last Supper with the apostles; where, after his resurrection, he appeared in their midst; where the Holy Spirit descended with power upon Mary and the disciples. Here the Church was born, and she was born *to go forth*. From here she *set out*, with the broken bread in her hands, the wounds of Christ before her eyes, and the Spirit of love in her heart.

In the Upper Room, the risen Jesus, sent by the Father, bestowed upon the apostles his own Spirit, and with his power he sent them forth to renew the face of the earth (see Psalm 104:30).

To go forth, to set out, does not mean to forget. The Church, in her going forth, preserves the *memory* of what took place here; the Spirit, the Paraclete, *reminds her* of every word and every action, and reveals their true meaning.

The Upper Room speaks to us of *service*, of Jesus giving the disciples an example by washing their feet. Washing one another's feet signifies welcoming, accepting, loving, and serving one another. It means serving the poor, the sick, and the outcast, those whom I find difficult, those who annoy me.

The Upper Room reminds us, through the Eucharist, of *sacrifice*. In every Eucharistic celebration Jesus offers himself for us to the Father, so that we too can be united with him, offering to God our lives, our work, our joys and our sorrows . . . offering everything as a spiritual sacrifice.

The Upper Room also reminds us of *friendship*. "No longer do I call you servants—Jesus said to the Twelve—but I have called you friends" (John 15:15). The Lord makes us his friends; he reveals God's will to us, and he gives us his very self. This is the most beautiful part of being a Christian and, especially, of being a priest: becoming a friend of the Lord Jesus, and discovering in our hearts that he is our friend.

The Upper Room reminds us of the Teacher's *farewell* and his *promise* to return to his friends: "When I go . . . I will come again and will take you to myself, that where I am you may be also" (John 14:3). Jesus does not leave us, nor does he ever abandon us. He precedes us to the house of the Father, where he desires to bring us as well.

The Upper Room, however, also reminds us of *pettiness*, of *curiosity*—"Who is the traitor?"—and of *betrayal*. We ourselves, and not just others, can reawaken those attitudes whenever we look at our brother or sister with contempt, whenever we judge them, whenever by our sins we betray Jesus.

The Upper Room reminds us of *sharing, fraternity, harmony,* and *peace* among ourselves. How much love and goodness has flowed from the Upper Room! How much charity has gone forth from here, like a river from its source, beginning as a stream and then expanding and becoming a great torrent. All the saints drew from this source; and hence the great river of the Church's holiness continues to flow: from the Heart of Christ, from the Eucharist, and from the Holy Spirit.

Lastly, the Upper Room reminds us of the birth of the *new family*, the Church, our holy Mother the hierarchical Church established by the risen Jesus; a family that has a Mother, the Virgin Mary. Christian families belong to this great family, and in it they find the light and strength to press on and be renewed, amid the challenges and difficulties of life. All God's children, of every people and language, are invited and called to be part of this great family, as brothers and sisters and sons and daughters of the one Father in heaven.

These horizons are opened up by the Upper Room, the horizons of the Risen Lord and his Church.

From here the Church goes forth, impelled by the life-giving breath of the Spirit. Gathered in prayer with the Mother of Jesus, the Church lives in constant expectation of a renewed outpouring of the Holy Spirit. Send forth your Spirit, Lord, and renew the face of the earth (Psalm 104:30)!

A Heart That Is Moved

AT THE BEGINNING OF LENT, it does us good as priests to reflect together on mercy. We all need it. Also the faithful, since as pastors we must extend great, great mercy!

The passage from the Gospel of Matthew that we heard makes us turn our gaze to Jesus as he goes about the cities and villages. And this is curious. Where was Jesus most often, where could he most easily be found? On the road. He seemed to be homeless, because he was always on the road. Jesus' life was on the road. He especially invites us to grasp the depths of his heart, what he feels for the crowds, for the people he encounters: that interior attitude of "compassion." Seeing the crowds, he felt compassion for them. For he saw the people were "harassed and helpless, like sheep without a shepherd." We have heard these words so many times that perhaps they do not strike us powerfully. But they are powerful! A little like the many people whom you meet today on the streets of your own neighborhoods. Then the horizon broadens, and we see that these towns and villages are not only Rome and Italy; they are the world, and those helpless crowds are the peoples of many nations who are suffering through even more difficult situations.

Thus we understand that we are not here to take part in a pleasant retreat at the beginning of Lent, but rather to hear the voice of the Spirit speaking to the whole Church of our time, which is the time of mercy. I am sure of this. It is not only Lent; we are living in a time of mercy, and have been for thirty years or more, up to today.

In the Church, Everything Is the Time of Mercy

This was an intuition of Saint John Paul II. He "sensed" that this was the time of mercy. We think of the beatification and canonization of Sr. Faustina Kowalska. On that occasion, John Paul II introduced the Feast of Divine Mercy. Little by little, he advanced and went forward on this.

In his homily for the canonization, which took place in 2000, John Paul II emphasized that the message of Jesus Christ to Sr. Faustina was located, in time, between the two World Wars and is intimately tied to the history of the twentieth century. And looking to the future he said, "What will the years ahead bring us? What will man's future on earth be like? We are not given to know. However, it is certain that in addition to new progress there will unfortunately be no lack of painful experiences. But the light of divine mercy, which the Lord in a way wished to return to the world through Sr. Faustina's charism, will illumine the way for the men and women of the third millennium" (*Homily*, Sunday, April 30, 2000). It is clear. Now it is explicit, but it was something that had been maturing in his heart for some time. Through his prayer, he had this intuition.

Today we forget everything far too quickly, even the Magisterium of the Church! Part of this is unavoidable, but we cannot forget the great content, the great intuitions and gifts that have been left to the People of God. And divine mercy is one of these. It is a gift that he gave to us, one that comes from above. It is up to us, as ministers of the Church, to keep this message alive, above all through preaching and in our actions, in signs and in pastoral choices, such as the decision to restore priority to the Sacrament of Reconciliation and to the works of mercy. Reconciliation, making peace through the sacrament, also with words, and with works of mercy.

What Does Mercy Mean for Priests?

It occurs to me that some of you have phoned, written letters, then spoke with me on the phone. "But Father, what have you got against priests?" They were saying that I bash priests! I do not wish to bash you here.

Let us ask ourselves what mercy means for a priest; allow me to speak for us priests. For us, for all of us! Priests are moved to compassion before the sheep, like Jesus, when he saw the people harassed and helpless, like sheep without a shepherd. Jesus has the "compassionate bowels" of God; Isaiah speaks about it very much: he is full of tenderness for the people, especially for those who are excluded, that is, for sinners, for the sick whom no one takes care of. Thus, in the image of the Good Shepherd, the priest is a man of mercy and compassion, close to his people and a servant to all. This is a pastoral criterion I would like to emphasize strongly: closeness. Closeness and service, but closeness, nearness! Whoever is wounded in life, in whatever way, can find in the priest attention and a sympathetic ear. The priest reveals a heart, especially in administering the Sacrament of Reconciliation; he reveals it by his whole attitude, by the manner in which he welcomes, listens, counsels, and absolves. But this comes from how he experiences the Sacrament firsthand, from how he allows himself to be embraced by God the Father in Confession and remains in this embrace. If one experiences this in one's own regard, in his own heart, he can also give it to others in his ministry. And I leave you with the question: How do I confess? Do I allow myself to be embraced? A great priest from Buenos Aires comes to mind; he is younger than I, around the age of seventy-two. He is a great confessor: there are always people waiting in line for him there. The majority of priests confess to him. And once he came to see me. "But

Father. . . ." "Tell me." "I have a small scruple, because I know that I forgive too much!" "Pray . . . if you forgive too much." And we spoke about mercy. At a certain point he said to me: "You know, when I feel this scruple keenly, I go to the chapel, before the Tabernacle, and I say to Him: Excuse me, but it's your fault, because it is you who has given me the bad example! And I go away at peace." It is a beautiful prayer of mercy! If one experiences this in his own Confession, in his own heart, he is able to give it to others.

The priest is called to learn this, to have a heart that is moved. Priests who are—allow me to say the word—"aseptic," those "from the laboratory," all clean and tidy, do not help the Church. Today we can think of the Church as a "field hospital." Excuse me, but I repeat it, because this is how I see it, how I feel it is: a "field hospital." Wounds need to be treated, so many wounds! So many wounds! There are so many people who are wounded by material problems, by scandals, also in the Church. People wounded by the world's illusions. We priests must be there, close to these people. Mercy first means treating the wounds. When someone is wounded, he needs this immediately, not tests to determine one's level of cholesterol and glycemic index. But there's a wound; treat the wound, and then we can look at the results of the tests. Then specialized treatments can be done, but first we need to treat the open wounds. I think this is what is most important at this time. And there are also hidden wounds, because there are people who distance themselves in order to avoid showing their wounds closer. . . . The custom comes to mind, in the Mosaic Law, of the lepers in Jesus' time, who were always kept at a distance in order not to spread the contagion. There are people who distance themselves through shame, through shame, so as not to let their wounds be seen. And perhaps they distance themselves with some bitterness against the Church, but deep down inside there is a wound. They want a caress! And you, dear brothers—I ask you—do you know the wounds of your parishioners? Do you perceive them? Are you close to them? It's the only question.

Mercy Means Neither Generosity nor Rigidity

Let us return to the Sacrament of Reconciliation. It often happens that we priests hear our faithful telling us they have encountered a very "strict" priest in the confessional, or a very "generous" priest, that is, a rigorist or a laxist. And this is not good. It is normal that there be differences in the style of confessors, but these differences cannot disregard the essential, that is, sound moral doctrine and mercy. Neither the laxist nor the rigorist bears witness to Jesus Christ, for neither the one nor the other takes care of the person he encounters. The rigorist washes his hands of them. In fact, he nails the person to the law, understood in a cold and rigid way; and the laxist also washes his hands of them: he is only apparently merciful, but in reality by minimizing the sin he does not take seriously the problems of that conscience. True mercy *takes the person into one's care*, listens to him attentively, approaches the situation with respect and truth, and accompanies him on the journey of reconciliation. And this is demanding, yes, certainly. The truly merciful priest behaves like the Good Samaritan, but why does he do it? Because his heart is capable of having compassion; it is the heart of Christ!

We are well aware that neither laxity nor rigorism fosters holiness. Perhaps some rigorists seem holy, holy. But think of Pelagius and then let's talk. Neither laxity nor rigorism sanctifies the priest, and they do not sanctify the faithful! However, mercy accompanies the journey of holiness; it accompanies it and makes it grow. Too much work for a parish priest? It is true, too much work! And how do we accompany and foster the journey of holiness? Through pastoral suffering, which is a form of mercy. What does pastoral suffering mean? It means suffering for and with the person. And this is not easy! Suffering like a father and mother suffer for their children; I venture to say, also with anxious concern.

To explain, I'll put to you some questions that help me when a priest comes to me. They also help me when I am alone before the Lord!

Tell me: Do you weep? Or have we lost our tears? I remember that in the old missals, those of another age, there is a most beautiful prayer to ask for the gift of tears. The prayer began like this: "Lord, who commanded Moses to strike the rock so that water might gush forth, strike the stone of my heart so that tears . . ."; the prayer went more or less like this. It was very beautiful. But, how many of us weep before the suffering of a child, before the breakup of a family, before so many people who do not find the path? The weeping of a priest. . . . Do you weep? Or in this priesthood have we lost all tears?

Do you weep for your people? Tell me, do you offer intercessory prayer before the Tabernacle?

Do you struggle with the Lord for your people, as Abraham struggled?

"Suppose they were fewer? Suppose there were twenty-five? And suppose they were twenty?" (Genesis 18:22–33). This courageous prayer of intercession. We speak of *parrhesia*, of apostolic courage, and we think of pastoral plans. This is good, but the same *parrhesia* is also needed in prayer. Do you struggle with the Lord? Do you argue with the Lord as Moses did? When the Lord was annoyed, tired of his people, he said to him: "Don't worry . . . I will destroy everything, and I will make you the head of another people." "No. No. If you destroy the people, destroy me too." These were real men! Do we have enough guts to struggle with God for our people?

I'll ask you another question: in the evening, how do you conclude your day? With the Lord or in front of the television? What is your relationship with those who help you to be more merciful? That is, what is your relationship with the children, with the elderly, with the sick? Do you know how to reassure them, or are you embarrassed to embrace an elderly person?

Do not be ashamed of the flesh of your brother. In the end, we will be judged on our ability to draw close to "all flesh"— as Isaiah says. Do not be ashamed of the flesh of your brother. "Making ourselves close": closeness, nearness, being close to the flesh of one's brother. The priest and the Levite who had passed by before the Good Samaritan did not know how to draw close to the person who had been beaten by bandits. Their hearts were closed. Perhaps the priest looked at his watch and said, "I have to go to Mass, I cannot be late for Mass," and he left. Excuses! How often we justify ourselves to get around the problem. The other, the Levite, or the doctor of the law, the lawyer, said, "No, I cannot because if I do this, tomorrow I will have to go and testify, I will lose time." Excuses! Their hearts were closed. But a closed heart always justifies itself for what it has not done. Instead, the Samaritan opens his heart; he allows his heart to be moved, and this interior movement translates into practical action, in a concrete and effective intervention to help another person.

At the end of time, only those who have not been ashamed of the flesh of their brother who is injured and excluded will be permitted to contemplate the glorified flesh of Christ.

I admit, sometimes it does me good to read the list on which I will be judged, it benefits me: it is contained in Matthew 25.

These are the things that came to my mind to share with you. It is a bit rough and ready as things came to mind. It will do us good.

In Buenos Aires—I am speaking of another priest—there was a well-known confessor: he was a Sacramentine. Almost all the priests confessed to him. On one of the two occasions he came, John Paul II requested a confessor at the Nunciature, and he went. He was old, very old. He had served as Provincial in his Order, as a professor . . . but always as a confessor, always. And a long line was always awaiting him in the Church of the Most Blessed Sacrament. At the time, I was Vicar General and was living in the Curia, and every morning, early, I would go down to the fax machine to see if anything was there. And on Easter morning I read a fax from the community superior: "Yesterday, a half hour before the Easter Vigil, Fr. Aristi died at the age of ninety-four—or ninety-six? The funeral will be on such and such a day." And on Easter morning I was to go to lunch with the priests at the retirement home—I usually did on Easter—and then, I said to myself, after lunch I will go to the Church. It was a large church, very large, with a beautiful crypt. I went down into the crypt and the coffin was there; only two old women were praying there, but not a single flower. I thought to myself: this man, who forgave the sins of all the clergy of Buenos Aires, including mine, not even a flower. I went up and went to a florist—because in Buenos Aires there are flower shops at the crossroads, on the streets, where there are people—and I bought flowers, roses. And I returned and began to decorate the coffin with flowers. I looked at the Rosary in his hands, and immediately it came to mind—because of the thief that we all have inside of us, don't we? And while I was arranging the flowers I took the cross off the Rosary, and with a little effort I detached it. At that moment I looked at him and said, "Give me half of your mercy." I felt something powerful that gave me the courage to do this and to say this prayer! And then I put the cross here, in my pocket. But the Pope's shirts don't have pockets, but I always carry it here in a little cloth bag, and that cross has been with me from that moment until today. And when a uncharitable thought against someone comes to mind, my hand always touches it here, always. And I feel the grace! I feel its benefit. What good the example of a merciful priest does, of a priest who draws close to wounds.

If you think about it, surely you have known many, many of them, because priests are good! They are good. I believe that it is not because of us who are bishops that we are strong; rather, it is because of the parish priests, the priests! It is true, this is true! It is not a little incense to comfort you; I truly believe it to be so.

Mercy. Think of the many priests who are in heaven and ask of them this grace! May they grant you the mercy they had with their faithful. This does good.

Thank you for having listened and for having come here.

Do You Love Me?

THE BIBLICAL READINGS we have heard make us think. They have made me think deeply. I have conceived of a sort of meditation for us bishops, first for me, a bishop like you, and I share it with you.

It is important—and I am particularly glad—that our first meeting should take place here, on the site that guards not only Peter's tomb but also the living memory of his witness of faith, his service to the Truth, and his gift of himself to the point of martyrdom for the Gospel and for the Church.

This evening, this Altar of the Confession thus becomes for us the Sea of Tiberias, on whose shores we listen once again to the marvelous conversation between Jesus and Peter with the question addressed to the Apostle, but which must also resonate in our own hearts, as bishops.

"Do you love me?" "Are you my friend?" (John 21:15ff.).

The question is addressed to a man who, despite his solemn declarations, let himself be gripped by fear and so had denied.

"Do you love me?" "Are you my friend?"

The question is addressed to me and to each one of us, to all of us: if we take care not to respond too hastily and superficially, it impels us to look within ourselves, to reenter ourselves.

"Do you love me?" "Are you my friend?"

The one who scrutinizes hearts (Romans 8:27) makes himself a beggar of love and questions us on the one truly essential issue, a premise and condition for feeding his sheep, his lambs, his Church. May every ministry be based on this intimacy with the Lord. Living with him is the measure of our ecclesial service, which is expressed in readiness to obey, to humble ourselves, as we heard in the Letter to the Philippians, and for the total gift of self (2:6–11).

Moreover, the consequence of loving the Lord is giving everything—truly everything, even our life—for him. This is what must distinguish our pastoral ministry; it is the litmus test that tells us how deeply we have embraced the gift received in responding to Jesus' call, and how closely bound we are to the individuals and communities that have been entrusted to our care. We are not the expression of a structure or of an organizational need. Even with the service of our authority we are called to be a sign of the presence and action of the Risen Lord—thus to build up the community in brotherly love.

Not that this should be taken for granted: even the greatest love, in fact, when it is not constantly nourished, weakens and fades away. Not for nothing did the Apostle Paul recommend: "Take heed to yourselves and to all the flock, of which the Holy Spirit has made you guardians, to feed the church of the Lord which he obtained with his own Son's blood" (Acts 20:28).

A lack of vigilance—as we know—makes a pastor tepid; it makes him absentminded, forgetful, and even impatient. It tantalizes him with the prospect of a career, the enticement of money, and with compromises with a mundane spirit. It makes him lazy, turning him into an official, a state functionary concerned with himself, with organization and structures, rather than with the true good of the People of God. Then one runs the risk of denying the Lord as did the Apostle Peter, even if he formally presents him and speaks in his name; such a one obscures the holiness of the hierarchical Mother Church, making her less fruitful.

Who are we, Brothers, before God? What are our trials? We have so many; each one of us has his own. What is God saying to us through them? What are we relying on in order to surmount them?

Just as it did Peter, Jesus' insistent and heartfelt question can leave us pained and more aware of the weakness of our freedom, threatened as it is by thousands of interior and exterior forms of conditioning that all too often give rise to bewilderment, frustration, and even disbelief.

These are not, of course, the sentiments and attitudes that the Lord wants to inspire; rather, the Enemy, the Devil, takes advantage of them to isolate us in bitterness, complaint, and despair.

Jesus, the Good Shepherd, does not humiliate or abandon people to remorse. Through him the tenderness of the Father, who consoles and revitalizes, speaks. It is he who brings us from the disintegration of shame—because shame truly breaks us up—to the fabric of trust; he restores courage, re-entrusts responsibility, and sends us out on mission.

Peter, purified in the crucible of forgiveness, could say humbly, "Lord, you know everything; you know that I love you" (John 21:17). I am sure that we can all say this with heartfelt feeling. And Peter, purified, urges us in his First Letter to tend "the flock of God . . . not by constraint but willingly, not for shameful gain but eagerly, not as domineering over those in your charge but by being examples to the flock" (1 Peter 5:2–3).

Yes, being pastors means believing every day in the grace and strength that come to us from the Lord, despite our weakness, and wholly assuming the responsibility for walking *before* the flock, relieved of the burdens that obstruct healthy apostolic promptness, hesitant leadership, so as to make our voice recognizable both to those who have embraced the faith and to those who "are not [yet] of this fold" (John 10:16). We are called to make our own the dream of God, whose house knows no exclusion of people or peoples, as Isaiah prophetically foretold (see Isaiah 2:2–5).

For this reason being pastors also means being prepared to walk *among* and *behind* the flock; being capable of listening to the silent tale of those who are suffering and of sustaining the steps of those who fear they may not make it; attentive to raising them up, to reassuring and to instilling hope. Our faith emerges strengthened from sharing with the lowly. Let us therefore set aside every form of arrogance to bend down to all whom the Lord has entrusted to our care. Among them let us keep a special, very special, place for our priests. Especially for them may our heart, our hand, and our door stay open in every circumstance. Our priests are the first faithful that we bishops have. Let us love them! Let us love them with all our heart! They are our sons and our brothers!

Dear brothers, the profession of faith we are now renewing together is not a formal act. Rather, it means renewing our response to the "Follow me" with which John's Gospel ends (21:19). It leads to living our lives in accordance with God's plan, committing our whole self to the Lord Jesus. The discernment that knows and takes on the thoughts, expectations, and needs of the people of our time stems from this.

In this spirit, I warmly thank each one of you for your service, for your love for the Church.

And the Mother is here! I place you, and myself, under the mantle of Mary, Our Lady.

Mother of silence, who watches over the mystery of God,
Save us from the idolatry of the present time,
    to which those who forget are condemned.
Purify the eyes of pastors with the eye wash of memory.
Take us back to the freshness of the origins,
    for a prayerful, penitent Church.
Mother of the beauty that blossoms from faithfulness
    to daily work,
Lift us from the torpor of laziness, pettiness, and defeatism.
Clothe pastors in the compassion that unifies,
    that makes whole.
Let us discover the joy of a humble, brotherly,
    serving Church.
Mother of tenderness, who envelops us in patience
    and mercy,
Help us burn away the sadness, impatience, and rigidity
    of those who do not know what it means to belong.
Intercede with your Son so that our hands, our feet,
    our hearts might be agile:
Let us build the Church with the Truth of love.
Mother, we shall be the People of God,
    pilgrims bound for the Kingdom. Amen.

When We Pray, We Are Fighting for Our People

MEDITATING ON THE READINGS for this Sunday (Genesis 18:20–32; Colossians 2:12–14; Luke 11:1–3) inspired me to write this letter. I don't know why, but I felt a strong urge to do so. At first there was a question: Do I pray? It then became, do we, priests and religious, pray? Do we pray enough? I had to answer this question about myself. By offering you this question, I hope that each of you will also be able to respond to it from the depths of your heart.

The quantity and quality of problems that we face every day lead us to action: providing solutions, planning, building. This fills most of our day. We are workers, laborers for the Kingdom, and we come home at night tired out by the energy expended. I believe that we can affirm objectively that we are not lazy. Much work is done. The succession of complaints, the urgency of the services we provide, exhaust us, and so our lives continue unfolding in the service of the Lord in the Church. Nonetheless, we do feel the burden, if not the distress, of a pagan society that proclaims its principles and so-called values with such audacity and self-assurance that it shakes our conviction in apostolic perseverance and even our real, concrete faith in the Lord, living and acting in the midst of human history, in the midst of the Church. At the end of the day, sometimes, we arrive in a sorry state, and, without realizing it, a certain diffuse pessimism seeps into our heart, shielding us in a "bunker" mentality and anointing us with a defeatist psychology that reduces us to defensive withdrawal. There our soul shrivels and becomes timid.

And so, between the intense and exhausting apostolic work, on the one hand, and the aggressively pagan culture, on the other, our hearts shrink in this practical powerlessness that leads us to a minimalist attitude of surviving in the hope of preserving the faith. However, we are not ignorant, and we know that something is missing in this picture, that the horizon has almost become a fence, that something is limiting our apostolic zeal in proclaiming the Kingdom. Could it not be that we are trying to do things alone, and we feel responsible, in an unfocused way, for finding solutions? We know that we cannot do it alone. Here the question arises: Are we leaving space for the Lord? Am I leaving time in my day for him to act? Or am I so busy doing things that I forget to let him enter?

I would imagine that poor Abraham was very frightened when God told him that he was going to destroy Sodom. For certain he thought of his relatives there, but he went even further: Would it not be possible to save these poor people? He starts to bargain. Despite the holy religious fear of being in the presence of God, a responsibility was imposed on Abraham. He felt responsible. Chafing at the order, he feels he has to intercede to save the situation; he feels that he has to struggle with God, to enter into a wrestling match. It is no longer just his relatives who interest him, but all these people; so he risks interceding. He engages in hand-to-hand struggle with God. He could have stayed quiet with his conscience after his first attempt, enjoying the promise of a son, which had just been made to him (Genesis 18:9), but he keeps going. Perhaps he already unconsciously thinks of these sinful people as his own children. I don't know, but he decides to risk himself for them.

His intercession is courageous, even at the risk of annoying the Lord. This is the courage of true intercession.

Several times I spoke of *parrhesia,* of courage and zeal in our apostolic activity. The same attitude has to characterize our prayer: prayer with *parrhesia.* We cannot be satisfied with asking only once; Christian intercession is loaded to the limit with our insistence. That was how David prayed for his dying son (2 Samuel 12:15–18), how Moses prayed for the rebellious people (Exodus 32:11–14; Numbers 4:10–19; Deuteronomy 9:18–20), leaving aside comfort and personal gain and the possibility of becoming leader of a great nation (Exodus 32:10). He didn't change "parties" or negotiate with his people; instead, he fought to the end. Our awareness of being chosen by the Lord for consecration or ministry should distance us from all indifference, comfort, or personal interest in the fight for this people from whom we have been drawn and to whom we are sent to serve. Like Abraham, we have to bargain with God with true courage for their salvation, and this is tiring, just as Abraham's arms became tired when he was in the midst of the battle (see Exodus 17:11–13). Intercession is not for the faint of heart. We don't pray to ease our conscience or to enjoy merely aesthetic inner harmony. When we pray, we are fighting for our people. Do I pray this way? Or do I become tired or bored or try not to get myself into this mess so that things go smoothly for me? Am I like Abraham in his courageous intercession, or do I end up in that pettiness of Jonah lamenting the leaky roof rather than those men and women who are victims of a pagan culture and "who do not know their right hand from their left" (Jonah 4:11).

In the Gospel, Jesus is clear: "Ask, and it will be given you; search and you will find; knock, and the door will be opened to you." And so we understand. He gives us the example of the man knocking on his neighbor's door at midnight for three loaves of bread, unconcerned that he may be perceived as rude; his only interest is to get food for his guest. And although her timing is bad, we see in that Canaanite woman (Matthew 15:21–28), who risks being sent away by the disciples (v. 23) and being called a "dog" (v. 27), what is required to get what she wants: the healing of her daughter. That woman really knew how to fight courageously in prayer.

For this perseverance and insistence in prayer the Lord promises the certainty of success: "Ask, and it will be given you; search and you will find; knock, and the door will be opened to you." And he explains the reason for this success: "Is there anyone among you who, if your child asks for a fish, will give a snake instead of a fish? Or if the child asks for an egg, will give a scorpion? If you, then, who are evil, know how to give good gifts to your children, how much more will the heavenly Father give the Holy Spirit to those who ask him!" The Lord's promise about trust and perseverance in prayer goes far beyond what we can imagine: in addition to what we ask for, he will give us the Holy Spirit. When Jesus exhorts us to pray insistently, he throws us into the very bosom of the Trinity, and through his sacred humanity, he brings us to the Father and he promises the Holy Spirit.

I return to the image of Abraham and the city he wanted to save. We are all aware of the pagan dimension of the culture we live in, a worldview that weakens our certainties and our faith. Daily we are witnesses of the intent of the powerful of this world to banish the living God and replace him with fashionable idols. We see how the abundance of life, which the Father offers us in creation and Jesus Christ in redemption, is replaced by the aptly named "culture of death." We also note how the Church's image is deformed and manipulated by disinformation, defamation, and slander, and how the sins and failures of her children are aired by the media as proof that she has nothing good to offer. For the media, holiness is not news, but scandal and sin certainly are. Who can fight as equals with that? Are any of us deluded that something can be done with merely human means, with Saul's armor? (See 1 Samuel 17:38–40.)

Be careful: our fight is not against human powers but against the powers of darkness (see Ephesians 6:12). As happened to Jesus (see Matthew 4:1–11), Satan will seek to seduce us, disorient us, offer "viable alternatives." We cannot allow ourselves the luxury of being gullible and complacent. It's true, we have to talk with all persons, but the temptation is not to communicate. We can only take refuge in the power of the God's Word, like the Lord did in the wilderness, and in recourse to begging in prayer: the prayer of the child, the poor, the simple, of the one who knows himself to be a child seeking his Father's help; the prayer of the humble, of the poor without resources. The humble have nothing to lose; indeed, the way is revealed to them (Matthew 11:25–26). We would do well to tell ourselves that it is not the time of the census, of triumph, and of harvest, that in our culture the enemy sows the weeds with the Lord's wheat, and that both grow together. Now is not the time for us to get used to this but rather to bend over and pick up the five stones for David's slingshot (see 1 Samuel 17:40). Now is the time to pray.

Some of you may think that I have gone apocalyptic or been seized by an attack of Manichaeism. Apocalyptic, yes, I would accept that, because the Book of Revelation is the book of the Church's daily life, and eschatology takes shape in every one of our attitudes. As for going Manichaean, I think not, because I am convinced that it is not our task to be separating the wheat from the weeds (the angels will do this on the day of harvest); if we can distinguish them, we will not be confused, and we will be able to defend the wheat. I ask myself, how would Mary live these daily contradictions, and how would she pray about them? What passed through her heart when she was returning from Ain Karim and the signs of maternity were already evident? What was she going to say to Joseph? How would she talk to God on the journey from Nazareth to Bethlehem, or on the flight to Egypt, or when Simeon and Anna spontaneously burst forth in that liturgy of praise, or that day when her son was left at the Temple, or at the foot of the Cross? Before these contradictions, and so many others, she prayed, and her heart became tired in the presence of the Father; she asked to be able to read and understand the signs of the times and to be able to care for the wheat. Speaking of this attitude, John Paul II says that Mary survived a certain "peculiar heaviness of the heart" (*Redemptoris mater*, 17). This prayer fatigue has nothing to do with the tiredness and boredom I referred to above.

And so we can say that prayer, even though it gives us peace and confidence, also fatigues our heart. It is the fatigue of those who do not deceive themselves, who maturely take on their pastoral responsibilities, who know that they are a minority in this "perverse and adulterous generation," and who accept to fight with God day in and day out to save their people. So here is the question: Do I have a heart fatigued in the courage of intercession; and, at the same time, in the midst of so much fighting, do I feel the serene peace of soul of one who moves in familiarity with God? Fatigue and peace go together in the heart that prays. Was I able to experience what it means to take seriously and to take charge of so many situations of pastoral work; and, while I do everything humanly possible to help, am

I interceding for God's people in prayer? Was I able to savor the simple experience of casting my burdens on the Lord (see Psalm 55:22) in prayer? How good it would be if we could understand and follow Saint Paul's advice: "Do not worry about anything, but in everything by prayer and supplication with thanksgiving let your requests be made known to God. And the peace of God, which surpasses all understanding, will guard your hearts and your minds in Christ Jesus" (Philippians 4:6–7).

These are more or less the things that I felt when meditating on the three readings for this Sunday, and I wanted to share them with you, the ones with whom I work in caring for God's faithful people. I ask the Lord to make us as prayerful as he was when he lived among us, and to make us strongly persistent before the Father. I ask the Holy Spirit to lead us into the Mystery of the Living God and to pray in our hearts. We have already won, as the second reading proclaims to us. Standing tall, affirmed in victory, I ask that we go forward (see Hebrews 10:39) in our apostolic work, entering more and more into that familiarity with God that we experience in prayer. I ask that we make *parrhesia* grow in action and prayer: adult men and women in Christ and children in our surrender; men and women working as hard as they can, hearts weary in prayer. This is what Jesus, who called us, wants of us. May he grant us the grace to understand that our apostolic work, our difficulties, our struggles are not merely human things that begin and end in us. "The battle is not yours but God's" (2 Chronicles 20:15), and this moves us to give more time to daily prayer.

And please don't stop praying for me, because I need it. May Jesus bless you and may the Blessed Virgin take care of you.

Shepherds with the Odor of Sheep

THE SOLEMNITY of Our Lady of Luján, patroness of Argentina, directs our hearts to what Jesus said before he died—"Here is your mother"—which reminds us, at the same time, of Mary's maternal warmth for us. "A humble image of your pure and spotless conception was miraculously left in the village of Luján as a sign of your maternal protection of the pilgrim people," who are to be "lifted by your hand" to the Lord (Preface of the Mass). Our Mother takes care of our humility and takes us by the hand. Our Mother, who, "raised to the glory of heaven, accompanies the pilgrim Church with maternal love, and with kindness guides its steps homeward until the glorious day of the Lord" (Preface of the Mass for the Feast of Holy Mary, Mother of the Church). Our Mother, who, throughout the journey, never ceases to repeat to us what she said at Cana: "Do whatever he tells you" (John 2:5).

So let us begin by contemplating our Mother of Luján, not in isolation but in the midst of her children. It would be good for us, as pastors, to place ourselves in the midst of this people to whom we belong, from whom we were chosen for service and, as God's faithful people, to draw nearer to the Mother. The people who continually flow to Luján and to the country's numerous other Marian shrines show us their needs, their search for God, their deepest wants and joys, and they ask us to help them to find, and to be found by, Jesus. Let us walk in their midst and ask for the grace to be "shepherds with the odor of sheep." It would be good for us to repeat, like an ejaculation, what the Collect implores: "Lord, look upon the faithfulness of your people," and to entreat the Father, as a people, to make us more faithful, more his children, more followers of Jesus.

This people looks to us and asks that we serve them in the mission for which we have been sent. We will look for the ways and the words to be able to realize today what Isaiah was proclaiming in the first reading: "Strengthen the weak hands, and make firm the feeble knees. Say to those who are of fearful heart, 'Be strong, do not fear! Here is your God!'" (Isaiah 35:3–4). It won't always be easy to proclaim these words. You have to seek, think, dialogue, and pray. This will produce in our lives as pastors that "peculiar heaviness of the heart" that, in the words of John Paul II, the Virgin suffered in her daily efforts to see the signs of God in the life of her Son (see *Redemptoris mater*, 17). As Jesus' first disciple, she opens the way of pastoral fatigue, that interior heaviness experienced by fathers and brothers who do not want to lose any of those who have been entrusted to them. Let's go back mentally to Luján and, in the midst of God's faithful people, with eyes raised to her, ask for the grace of this interior heaviness that anoints us in the cross of every day, often in the grey areas that are difficult to understand or in the darkness that makes our hope falter.

However, this hope cannot be negotiated because "we have also obtained an inheritance, having been destined . . . so that we, who were the first to set our hope on Christ, might live for the praise of his glory" (Ephesians 1:11–12), as we heard in the second reading. We look again to our Mother, who, throughout the history of peoples since Cana, drew near to her children in the most varied situations to plant hope in our hearts. We ask her for the grace to be pastors of hope who are not stifled by conflicts and hardships; to be pastors like Paul who, despite "disputes without and fears within" (2 Corinthians 7:5), did not stop proclaiming Jesus Christ, even at the cost of his own life: a priceless and daily martyr's proclamation. We ask her for the grace to believe firmly in "the hope that does not disappoint" (Roman's 5:5) and to be able to pass on this faith to our people. This hope makes us look ahead and repeat the words of Isaiah that we just heard: "Then the eyes of the blind shall be opened, and the ears of the deaf unstopped; then the lame shall leap like a deer, and the tongue of the speechless sing for joy. For waters shall break forth in the wilderness, and streams in the desert" (Isaiah 35:5–7).

Mother, present in the midst of your people—

Mother fatigued by your discipleship and following of Jesus Christ—

Mother of hope.

So we contemplate her, silent and eliciting filial smiles in the souls of her children. So we want to contemplate her with the confident petition of knowing how, and being able, to walk with her, in the midst of God's faithful people to whom we belong and whom we serve: the petition to make our hearts weary as we seek the signs of God in history and the grace to be men of hope. With these wishes let us look to her again, put ourselves near to her and, with her, pray to the Father, "Lord, look on the faithfulness of your people."

Do the People Leave Us Looking Like They Heard the Good News?

THIS MORNING I HAVE THE JOY of celebrating my first Chrism Mass as the Bishop of Rome. I greet all of you with affection, especially you, dear priests, who, like myself, today recall the day of your ordination.

The readings and the Psalm of our Mass speak of God's "anointed ones": the Suffering Servant of Isaiah, King David, and Jesus our Lord. All three have this in common: the anointing that they received was meant in turn to anoint God's faithful people, whose servants they are; they were anointed for the poor, for prisoners, for the oppressed. . . . A fine image of this "being for" others can be found in Psalm 133:2: "It is like the precious oil upon the head, running down upon the beard, on the beard of Aaron, running down upon the collar of his robe." The image of spreading oil, flowing down from the beard of Aaron upon the collar of his sacred robe, is an image of the priestly anointing, which, through Christ, the Anointed One, reaches the ends of the earth, represented by the robe.

The sacred robes of the high priest are rich in symbolism. One such symbol is that the names of the children of Israel were engraved on the onyx stones mounted on the shoulder pieces of the ephod, the ancestor of our present-day chasuble: six on the stone of the right shoulder piece and six on that of the left (see Exodus 28:6–14). The names of the twelve tribes of Israel were also engraved on the breastplate (see Esther 28:21). This means that the priest celebrates by carrying on his shoulders the people entrusted to his care and bearing their names written in his heart. When we put on our simple chasuble, it might well make us feel, upon our shoulders and in our hearts, the burdens and the faces of our faithful people, our saints and martyrs who are numerous in these times.

From the beauty of all these liturgical things, which is not so much about trappings and fine fabrics as about the glory of our God resplendent in his people, alive and strengthened, we turn now to a consideration of activity, action. The precious oil that anoints the head of Aaron does more than simply lend fragrance to his person; it overflows down to "the edges." The Lord will say this clearly: his anointing is meant for the poor, prisoners, and the sick, for those who are sorrowing and alone. My dear brothers, the ointment is not intended just to make us fragrant, much less to be kept in a jar, for then it would become rancid . . . and the heart bitter.

A good priest can be recognized by the way his people are anointed: this is a clear proof. When our people are anointed with the oil of gladness, it is obvious: for example, when they leave Mass looking as if they have heard good news. Our people like to hear the Gospel preached with "unction"; they like it when the Gospel we preach touches their daily lives, when it runs down like the oil of Aaron to the edges of reality, when it brings light to moments of extreme darkness, to the "out-skirts" where people of faith are most exposed to the onslaught of those who want to tear down their faith. People thank us because they feel that we have prayed over the realities of their everyday lives, their troubles, their joys, their burdens, and their hopes. And when they feel that the fragrance of the Anointed One, of Christ, has come to them through us, they feel encouraged to entrust to us everything they want to bring before the Lord: "Pray for me, Father, because I have this problem"; "Bless me, Father"; "Pray for me"—these words are the sign that the anointing has flowed down to the edges of the robe, for it has turned into a prayer of supplication, the supplication of the People of God. When we have this relationship with God and with his people, and grace passes through us, then we are priests, mediators between God and men. I want to emphasize that we need constantly to stir up God's grace and perceive in every request, even those requests that are inconvenient and at times purely material or downright banal—but only apparently so—the desire of our people to be anointed with fragrant oil, since they know that we have it. To perceive and to sense, even as the Lord sensed the hope-filled anguish of the woman suffering from hemorrhages when she touched the hem of his garment. At that moment, Jesus, surrounded by people on every side, embodied all the beauty of Aaron vested in priestly raiment, with the oil running down upon his robes. It is a hidden beauty, one that shines forth only for those faith-filled eyes of the woman troubled with an issue of blood. But not even the disciples—future priests—see or understand. On the "existential outskirts," they see only what is on the surface: the crowd pressing in on Jesus from all sides (Luke 8:42). The Lord, on the other hand, feels the power of the divine anointing that runs down to the edge of his cloak.

We need to "go out," then, in order to experience our own anointing, its power and its redemptive efficacy: to the "outskirts" where there is suffering, bloodshed, blindness that longs for sight, and prisoners in thrall to many evil masters. It is not in soul searching or constant introspection that we encounter the Lord. Self-help courses can be useful in life, but to live our priestly life going from one course to another, from one method to another, leads us to become Pelagians and to minimize the power of grace, which comes alive and flourishes to the extent that we, in faith, go out and give ourselves and the Gospel to others, giving what little ointment we have to those who have nothing, nothing at all.

The priest who seldom goes out of himself, who anoints little—I won't say "not at all" because, thank God, the people take the oil from us anyway—misses out on the best of our people, on what can stir the depths of his priestly heart. These are the ones who do not go out of themselves, and instead of being mediators, they gradually become intermediaries, managers. We know the difference: the intermediary, the manager, "has already received his reward," and since he doesn't put his own skin and his own heart on the line, he never hears a warm, heartfelt word of thanks. This is precisely the reason for the dissatisfaction of some, who end up sad—sad priests—in some sense becoming collectors of antiques or novelties instead of being shepherds living with "the odor of the sheep." This I ask you: be shepherds, with the "odor of the sheep"; make it real, as shepherds among your flock, fishers of men. True enough, the so-called crisis of priestly identity threatens us all and adds to the broader cultural crisis; but if we can resist its onslaught, we will be able to put out in the name of the Lord and cast our nets. It is not a bad thing that reality itself forces us to "put out into the deep," where what we are by grace is clearly seen as pure grace, out into the deep of the contemporary world, where the only thing that counts is "unction"—not function—and where the nets that overflow with fish are those cast solely in the name of the one in whom we have put our trust: Jesus. Dear lay faithful, be close to your priests with affection and with your prayers, that they may always be shepherds according to God's heart.

Dear priests, may God the Father renew in us the Spirit of holiness with whom we have been anointed. May he renew his Spirit in our hearts, that this anointing may spread to everyone, even to those "outskirts" where our faithful people most look for it and most appreciate it. May our people sense that we are the Lord's disciples; may they feel that their names are written upon our priestly vestments and that we seek no other identity; and may they receive through our words and deeds the oil of gladness that Jesus, the Anointed One, came to bring us. Amen.

The Grace of Apostolic Audacity

OUR PASTORAL CONCERN with "caring for our people's fragility" leads us to pray to the Lord and to ask with the simplicity of servants: Where are we bringing the fragility that we set out to find and that we are taking care of? What is the grace that we should ask for in order to take good care of the most vulnerable, your favored ones?

Today we bring into our hearts the look of the Lord, who, moved, stopped on many occasions to contemplate the people's fragility. Jesus' warm compassion was not self-absorbed or paralyzing, as often happens with us, but the contrary: it was a compassion that moved him to go out of himself with power and boldness to proclaim, to send out on mission, to send out to heal, as the Gospel passage we have just finished reading says.

Here we consider the Lord boldly assuming the mission to evangelize. Notice the verbs that he takes from Isaiah: "proclaim" (*euangelizein*) and "preach" (*keruzein*), two actions empowered by the Spirit that anointed him for mission. Note, for example, what he says of the "oppressed": this is not simply about freeing captives. The Gospel says that the Lord comes "to send them (*aposteilai*) on mission freed from their enslavement." And from among those who formerly were captives, the Lord chooses his envoys. Our Lord Jesus Christ erupts in our history—marked by vulnerability—with unstoppable dynamism, full of power and courage. This is kerygma, the core of our preaching: the resounding proclamation of that eruption in our history of Jesus Christ incarnated, dead, and risen.

In the diagnosis that Jesus makes of the world's situation there is nothing plaintive, nothing paralyzing; on the contrary, it is an invitation to fervent action. And the greatest boldness consists precisely in what is an inclusive action, in what connects him to the poorest, the oppressed, the blind . . . to the Father's little ones: connecting them by making them participants in the Good News, participants in his new vision of things, participants in the mission to include others once they have been set free. We could say, in our contemporary language, that Jesus' look is a "welfare-oriented" vision. The Lord does not come to heal the blind so that they can see the media spectacle of the world, but so they can see the wonders that God performs in the midst of his people. The Lord does not come to let the oppressed go free—from their faults and those of unjust structures—so that they feel better, but to send them on mission. The Lord does not proclaim a year of grace so that each of us, cured of affliction, can take a sabbatical year, but so that we, with him in the midst of us, can live our lives actively participating in all that creates our dignity as children of the living God.

The Lord, when he looks at our fragility, invites us to care for it not with fear but with boldness. "But take courage; I have conquered the world." "I am with you always, to the end of the age." This is why Peter's awareness of his own fragility, which he humbly confessed, does not elicit an invitation from the Lord to withdraw; rather, the Lord is moved to send him on mission, to exhort him to set out into the deep, to dare him to be a fisher of people. The magnitude of the faithful people's vulnerability, which fills the Lord with compassion, does not lead to a prudent calculation of our limited possibilities, such as the apostles suggested to him; rather, he urges them to trust without limits, to evangelical generosity and extravagance, as happened in the multiplication of the loaves. The sending out by the risen Lord, which is the crowning of the Gospel, is consistent with today's text, which is inaugural: "Go therefore and make disciples of all nation, baptizing them . . . and teaching them to obey everything that I have commanded you" (Matthew 28:19).

Apostolic audacity and courage are constitutive of mission. The ability to speak boldly is the mark of the Spirit, testimony to the authenticity of the kerygma and the proclamation of the Gospel. This is the attitude of "inner freedom" to say openly what has to be said; that healthy pride that leads us to "glory" in the Gospel that we are proclaiming; that unquenchable trust in the fidelity of Christ's witness that gives his witnesses the certainty that nothing "will be able to separate us from the love of God" (Romans 8:38ff.). If we pastors have this attitude, then the fragility of our people is well cared for and guided. This, then, is the grace that we want to ask of the Lord so that we can take care of the fragility of our people: the grace of apostolic audacity—strong, zealous audacity in the Spirit.

We humbly and confidently ask Our Lady for this grace— she who has been called "the first evangelizer." She, the joyous mother who delivers us to Christ, the one who exhorts us "to do whatever Jesus commands us." She is the first to experience interiorly the joy of setting out to evangelize and to participate in the unprecedented audacity of the Son and of contemplating and proclaiming how God "has shown strength with his arm; he has scattered the proud in the thoughts of their hearts. He has brought down the powerful from their thrones, and lifted up the lowly; he has filled the hungry with good things, and sent the rich away empty." From this audacity of Mary we are invited to participate as priests of the holy Church. To this sphere of evangelical joy—which is where our strength lies—we should lead the fragility of our people that we set out to find. That is the Good News: that we who are poor, fragile, vulnerable, and small have been looked upon, like her, with kindness and are part of the people over which is extended, from generation to generation, the mercy of the God of our ancestors.

With Hearts Burning from Within

Those who love me will keep my word, and my Father will love them.

Y EAR AFTER YEAR the Church calls us together for the Mass of Holy Thursday with this passage from the Gospel of Luke: "When he came to Nazareth, where he had been brought up, he went to the synagogue on the Sabbath day, as was his custom. He stood up to read, and the scroll of the prophet Isaiah was given to him" (Luke 4:16–17). I want to pause for a while to contemplate with you, dear brothers in the priesthood, this scene: this very descriptive scene portrays Jesus in his village synagogue, Jesus, as it were, in the neighborhood church, in our parish. It would be good to put ourselves in that scene imagining that small chapel in Nazareth, and—why not?—each one of us imagining Jesus in our parish, in our church.

If we look at what Jesus does, we see that the ritual of reading is still current. As at Mass when one stands up and goes to the lectern, they bring Jesus the book, and the attendant indicates the page to him. The Lord gets up, reads from Isaiah, returns the scroll to the attendant, and sits down. Simple rituals speak to us of family traditions, of Saturdays in the synagogue, of the hand of Joseph and of the Virgin, decisive gestures of Jesus that refer us to parish life. The image of the adult Jesus in the synagogue is paralleled in Luke with that of the child lost and found in the Temple, which they also attended "as usual" (Luke 2:42). Luke, as we know, has the life of Jesus revolve around the Temple of Jerusalem, from the declaration of Zachariah to the final image of those who form the new community after the Ascension: "they were continually in the temple blessing God" (Luke 24:53).

This great image of the relationship of the Lord with the Temple has corresponding images in daily life: these other images, those of the small village synagogues, are typified in the synagogue at Capernaum. A typical day begins when Jesus cures the man with the unclean spirit and then goes to the home of Peter—the rock of the Church—and when they open the door at sunset they are met by a crowd that pours through to be cured by Jesus (Luke 4:40). And these emergencies, as we say in our jargon, would at times take over the day. It is in the synagogue where Jesus, stalked by the Pharisees, healed the man with the withered hand (Luke 6:6), where he received the friends of the centurion who had built the village synagogue (Luke 7:1–10). Leaving the synagogue he cures the woman suffering from hemorrhages and the daughter of Jairus, the leader of the synagogue (Luke 8:49–56). In the synagogue he straightened up the woman who was bent over so that she could again praise God with dignity (Luke 13:10–17).

This is the image that I want to highlight today: that of Jesus in the middle of the faithful people of God, that of Jesus as priest and good shepherd in the middle of the universal and local Church. Because in this image is the force of our priestly identity. The Lord wants to keep on being, through us, his priests, in the middle of his faithful people (of which we are a part). He needs us to celebrate the Eucharist and to walk with the Church: that Church that is the great sanctuary that calls together the entire faithful people of God and, at the same time, the small chapel in which the life of every community comes into being; that Church that is the holy place in the middle of the cities where the Father keeps calling together those who want to worship him in Spirit and in truth.

It is good for us to think about Jesus surrounded by all the people we see every day in our churches; we never lack for persons in the community who come together to worship God, nor for the person who is not completely healthy in body or soul, nor the beggar with the empty hand, nor the bent-over woman, nor the hemorrhaging persons who know enough to touch the Lord's robe; there is no lack of those who perhaps do not practice, like the centurion, but who help with their alms and their good will; there is no lack of people who come to listen to the Word and who pray to, are amazed by, and praise God, nor is there a lack of those who are scandalized, those who come to gossip, the Pharisees who are always stalking everybody with their rules lacking in charity. Nor are we lacking holy old people like Simeon and Anna in our churches, children who stay after hours to learn the catechism. And quite frequently the Pharisee and the publican come in to pray; and every day, although only Jesus sees it, some widow places her last two coins in the poor box.

How does this Jesus, who enters the synagogue and prays "as usual," appeal to us? This Jesus who walks with the people in the processions and lines up among sinners so that John may baptize him; this Jesus who celebrates the Passover and who is immersed in the traditions of his people, transforming them from the inside? People realized that everything around him was renewed. Thus, we find this very remarkable contradiction between exultant praise and blasphemies poisoned by hatred before anyone who says only that this scripture has been fulfilled today. What is this telling us priests about what we are invited to?

We are invited to be men of the Church, which is the most contemporary translation—and the most contested—of "the imitation and following of Christ." Today, as then, the Lord is inviting us to be in the midst of our faithful people, soaked in their traditions and customs, without pretensions or outward, learned elitisms of any kind, and with hearts that burn from within so that the Holy Spirit renews the face of the earth and lights the fire that this same Lord brought.

We are invited to be priests who experience the Church as Mother, priests who are in love with the Holy and Immaculate Church, the true Spouse of Christ, and who do not lose the expectant look of first love. Priests capable of seeing and feeling the Catholic Church as one and the same, both in the major celebrations and in the hidden ones of the confessional. Priests with a heart open like that of the Church to welcome all, most especially and with all the tenderness possible, those our society excludes and forgets, confirming them in their dignity as children whom the Father loves. Priests who first correct the Church in themselves, asking pardon for their sins and nourishing themselves with the Eucharist and the Word, and who shortly thereafter, dare, fraternally as the Gospel says, to correct something in others, without ever "throwing pearls before swine," who seize upon our indiscrete handling of wounds and discord to harm and mock our Mother the Church. Priests who creatively and tirelessly call together those whom the Father attracts and brings near to his Son. Priests who go out to look for those whom Jesus loves to bring them back to the flock.

Priests who bring to the world the Spirit that sanctifies and builds the Church, and who do not allow their lives to become spiritually mundane.

I will end with an event that is a little further on in this Gospel text. It is striking that those who move from praise to hate to the point of wanting to do away with the Lord begin by wondering, "Is this not Joseph's son?" Their acquaintance with Jesus and his family distances them from God-made-flesh. And, conversely, the customs of his people did not distance Jesus from the Father or from his brothers—quite the contrary!

Today I wish to ask the Virgin and Saint Joseph, who know how to inculcate in Jesus this love for the ancient assembly of Israel and its customs, that our love of the Church in all her children and in all things have this family aspect. We priests especially ask Mary that we may see her face and think of her mother's heart when we speak of the Church and when we attend to the smallest of her children; that we feel that what we say about the Church we are saying about her; that what the Lord wants to do in us, the Church, are the same marvels he did in her. We ask for the grace that our priesthood and the Church may make the faithful people of God feel as loved as Mary loves them.

Evangelical Openness

IN A FEW WEEKS the Advent season will begin. This year it will be the liturgical start toward the Jubilee. The desire to let ourselves be visited by the Lord at his coming takes on a special significance in light of this event. On Christmas day, the Holy Doors will be opened, and, already anticipating this gesture, the Pope's oft-repeated invitation is resounding in my heart: "Open the doors to the Redeemer" (*Aperite portas,* 1). "Open the door to Christ" (*Redemptoris missio,* 3, 39). We must meet the birth of the Lord "like those who are waiting for their master . . . so that they may open the door for him" (Luke 12:36). This letter that I am writing to you is born of my desire to exhort you, as pastor and brother, to open your doors to the Lord: the door of your heart, the doors of your mind, the doors of our churches . . . every door. To open doors is a Christian task, a priestly task.

As we read in the Gospel, Jesus did that. At the beginning of his mission, he is presented opening the scroll of the prophet Isaiah (see Luke 4:17); and the Book of Revelation ends in a similar way: like the slaughtered Lamb, like the Lion of Judah, he is the only one "worthy to open the scroll and break its seal" (Revelation 5:2). The risen Jesus is he who "opened their [the disciples'] minds" on the way to Emmaus so they could "understand the scriptures" and remember: "Were our hearts not burning within us . . . while he was opening the scriptures to us?" (Luke 24:32). Many miracles were performed to bring about openness to the Word: Jesus touched the eyes of the two blind men "and their eyes were opened" (Matthew 9:30). To the deaf man with the speech impediment, Jesus said, "'Ephphatha,' that is, 'Be opened.' And immediately his ears were opened" (Mark 7:34). When Jesus "opens his mouth," it is the Kingdom of Heaven that is opened in the parables. "And opening his mouth, he began to teach them" (Matthew 5:2); "I will open my mouth in parables" (Matthew 13:35). When Jesus humbles himself and is baptized, when he prays (Luke 3:21), the sky opens and the loving voice of the father resounds: "This is my Son, the Beloved" (Matthew 3:16). And it is the same Lord who exhorts us: "Ask . . . and it will be opened to you" (Luke 11:9), and the Church asks "that God will open to us a door for the Word" (Colossians 4:3) because if Jesus opens the door "no one will shut it" (Revelation 3:7). The clear and definitive invitation that concentrates in an entirely personal way all the Lord's gestures of openness is found in the letter to the Church in Laodicea: "If . . . you open the door, I will come in to you and eat with you, and you with me" (Revelation 3:20).

Nowadays, openness is considered a value, although it is not always well understood. People say, "He is an open priest," contrasting him to "a closed priest." Like any evaluation, it depends on who makes it. At times, in a superficial evaluation, openness may mean "one who lets anything go" or "who is streetwise," or who is not "stiff-necked" or "rigid." But behind these comments that only touch the surface, there is always something hidden deep down that the people perceive. An open priest is he who "is able to listen while remaining true to his convictions." A man of the people once defined a priest in a simple phrase: "A priest is a man who talks to everybody." The priest is no respecter of persons, he implied. He was drawing attention to the fact that a priest is a person who can talk "well" with everyone, and he was clearly distinguishing him from those who speak well only with some, as well as from those who speak with everyone and say yes to everything.

Openness goes together with faithfulness. A characteristic of faithfulness is this single movement by which, on the one hand, the door to the heart is completely opened to the beloved person, and, on the other, this same door is closed to anyone who threatens this love. Opening the door to the Lord means opening the door to those he loves: the poor, young children, those who have strayed, sinners . . . in the end, all persons. It also means closing oneself to "idols": easy adulation, worldly success, lust, power, wealth, defamation, and—in the measure in which these anti-values are embodied—persons who want to enter our heart or our community to impose them.

Besides being faithful, the attitude of opening or closing the door has to be testimonial. This means testifying that, on the final day, there will be a door that is opened to some: the blessed of the Father, those who gave food and drink to "the least of these," those who had oil for their lamps, those who put the Word into practice . . . and closed to others: those who did not open their hearts to those in need, those who left their oil behind, those who said "Lord, Lord" with words but did not love with deeds.

Thus, openness is not a question of words but of gestures. The people understand by speaking of the priest who "always is" or "never is" (charitably prefacing this with "I already know that you are very busy, Father, because you have so many things . . ."). Evangelical openness plays out in places of entry: at the doors of the churches that, in this world where shopping malls never close, cannot stay closed for long, though it may be necessary to pay for surveillance and go down to the confessional more often; in the door that is the telephone, tiring and inconvenient in our world of hypercommunication, but that cannot remain for many hours at the mercy of the automatic answering machine. But these doors are rather exterior and mediated. They are an expression of that other door that is our face, our eyes, our smile, speeding up the pace and daring us to look at what we know is waiting. . . . In the confessional one knows that half the battle is won or lost in the greeting, in the manner of receiving the penitent, especially the one who gives that little look or makes that gesture that says, "May I?" An open, cordial, and warm reception succeeds in opening a soul to what the Lord already did peeping through the small viewing window. In contrast, a cold, rushed, or bureaucratic reception closes what was half-open. We know that we confess in different ways, depending on the priest who touches us, and this is true of the people too.

A beautiful image to examine our openness is the home. Some homes are open because they are "at peace," and hospitable because of their warmth. Not so neat that one is afraid to sit down (let alone smoke or eat anything) or so messy that they are embarrassing from outside. The same thing is true of the heart: the heart that has space for the Lord has space for others too. If there is no space and time for the Lord, then for others the place is reduced to fit its own temper, enthusiasm, or fatigue. And the Lord is like the poor: he draws near without our calling him, and he insists a little, but he does not stay if we do not stop him from going. It is easy to get rid of him. It is enough to move a little more quickly, as happens to beggars, or to look the other way when the children confront us in the subway.

Yes, openness to others goes hand in hand with our openness to the Lord. Only he, the one with the open heart, can open a space of peace in our heart, that peace that makes us hospitable to others. This is the role of the risen Jesus: to enter the closed upper room that, in any house, is the image of the heart, and open it by taking away all fear and filling the disciples with peace. At Pentecost, the Spirit seals the house and hearts of the apostles with this peace and transforms them into a house open to all, into the Church. The Church is like the open house of the merciful Father. Thus, our attitude must be that of the Father and not of the sons in the parable: neither that of the younger son, who makes use of the openness to escape, nor that of the narrow-minded older son, who believes he is looking after the inheritance better than his father.

Open the doors to the Lord! It is the request that I want to make today to all the priests. Open your doors! Those of your heart and those of your churches. Do not be afraid! Open them in the morning, in your prayer, in order to receive the Spirit who will fill you with peace and joy, and then go out to guide the faithful People of God. Open them during the day so that the prodigal children feel that you are waiting for them. Open them in the evening so that the Lord does not pass by and leave you in your solitude without entering and eating with you and keeping you company.

And always remember the one who is the Door of Heaven; the one with the heart opened by the sword, who understands all pain; the little servant of the Father who knew how to open herself completely to praise; the one who came out of herself and "hastened" to visit and comfort; the one who knows how to transform any small cave into the home of "God with us" with a few little cloths and a mountain of tenderness; the one who is always watching that we do not run out of wine in our lives; the one who knows to wait outside to make space for the Lord to instruct the people; the one who is always in the open field in any place where people are raising a cross and crucifying their children. Our Lady is our Mother, and, like any mother, she knows how to open the hearts of her children: all hidden sin is pardoned by God through her favor; all fickleness and confinement dissolve before her word; all fear about our mission dissipates if she accompanies us along the way.

I ask that She bless all of us and, with a mother's tenderness, continue to teach us each day to open the doors to the Redeemer.

Primary Features of Priestly Joy

IN THE ETERNAL "TODAY" of Holy Thursday, when Christ showed his love for us to the end (John 13:1), we recall the happy day of the institution of the priesthood, as well as the day of our own priestly ordination. The Lord anointed us in Christ with the oil of gladness, and this anointing invites us to accept and appreciate this great gift: the gladness, the joy of being a priest. Priestly joy is a priceless treasure, not only for the priest himself but for the entire faithful people of God: that faithful people from whom he is called to be anointed and which he, in turn, is sent to anoint.

Anointed with the oil of gladness so as to anoint others with the oil of gladness. Priestly joy has its source in the Father's love, and the Lord wishes the joy of this love to be "ours" and to be "complete" (John 15:11). I like to reflect on joy by contemplating Our Lady, for Mary, the "Mother of the living Gospel, is a wellspring of joy for God's little ones" (*Evangelii gaudium*, 288). I do not think it is an exaggeration to say that a priest is very little indeed: the incomparable grandeur of the gift granted us for the ministry sets us among the least of men. The priest is the poorest of men unless Jesus enriches him by his poverty, the most useless of servants unless Jesus calls him his friend, the most ignorant of men unless Jesus patiently teaches him as he did Peter, the frailest of Christians unless the Good Shepherd strengthens him in the midst of the flock. No one is more "little" than a priest left to his own devices; and so our prayer of protection against every snare of the Evil One is the prayer of our Mother: I am a priest because he has regarded my humility (see Luke 1:48). And in that humility we find our joy. Joy in our humility!

For me, there are three significant features of our priestly joy. It is a joy that *anoints us* (not one that "greases" us, making us unctuous, sumptuous, and presumptuous), it is a joy that is *imperishable,* and it is a *missionary* joy that spreads and attracts, starting backward—with those farthest from us.

A joy that anoints us. In a word: it has penetrated deep within our hearts; it has shaped them and strengthened them sacramentally. The signs of the ordination liturgy speak to us of the Church's maternal desire to pass on and share with others all that the Lord has given us: the laying on of hands, the anointing with sacred chrism, the clothing with sacred vestments, the first consecration that follows immediately. . . . Grace fills us to the brim and overflows, fully, abundantly and entirely in each priest. We are anointed down to our very bones . . . and our joy, which wells up from deep within, is the echo of this anointing.

An imperishable joy. The fullness of the gift, which no one can take away or increase, is an unfailing source of joy: an imperishable joy that the Lord has promised no one can take from us (John 16:22). It can lie dormant or be clogged by sin or by life's troubles, yet deep down it remains intact, like the embers of a burnt log beneath the ashes, and it can always be renewed. Paul's exhortation to Timothy remains ever timely: I remind you to fan into flame the gift of God that is within you through the laying on of my hands (see 2 Timothy 1:6).

A missionary joy. I would like especially to share with you and to stress this third feature: priestly joy is deeply bound up with God's holy and faithful people, for it is an eminently missionary joy. Our anointing is meant for anointing God's holy and faithful people: for baptizing and confirming them, healing and sanctifying them, blessing, comforting and evangelizing them.

And since this joy is one that springs up only when the shepherd is in the midst of his flock (for even in the silence of his prayer, the shepherd who worships the Father is with his sheep), it is a "guarded joy," watched over by the flock itself. Even in those gloomy moments when everything looks dark and a feeling of isolation takes hold of us, in those moments of listlessness and boredom that at times overcome us in our priestly life (and which I too have experienced), even in those moments God's people are able to "guard" that joy; they are able to protect you, to embrace you, and to help you open your heart to find renewed joy.

A "guarded joy": one guarded by the flock but also guarded by three sisters who surround it, tend it, and defend it: sister poverty, sister fidelity, and sister obedience.

The joy of priests is a joy that is sister to poverty. The priest is poor in terms of purely human joy. He has given up so much! And because he is poor, he, who gives so much to others, has to seek his joy from the Lord and from God's faithful people. He doesn't need to try to create it for himself. We know that our people are very generous in thanking priests for their slightest blessing and especially for the sacraments. Many people, in speaking of the crisis of priestly identity, fail to realize that identity presupposes belonging. There is no identity—and consequently joy of life—without an active and unwavering sense of belonging to God's faithful people (see *Evangelii gaudium*, 268). The priest who tries to find his priestly identity by soul searching and introspection may well encounter nothing more than "exit" signs, signs that say: exit from yourself, exit to seek God in adoration, go out and give your people what was entrusted to you, for your people will make you feel and taste who you are, what your name is, what your identity is, and they will make you rejoice in the hundredfold that the Lord has promised to those who serve him. Unless you "exit" from yourself, the oil grows rancid, and the anointing cannot be fruitful. Going out from ourselves presupposes self-denial; it means poverty.

Priestly joy is a joy that is sister to fidelity. Not primarily in the sense that we are all "immaculate" (would that by God's grace we were!), for we are sinners, but in the sense of an ever-renewed fidelity to the one Bride, to the Church. Here fruitfulness is key. The spiritual children that the Lord gives each priest, the children he has baptized, the families he has blessed and helped on their way, the sick he has comforted, the young people he catechizes and helps to grow, the poor he assists—all these are the "Bride" whom he rejoices to treat as his supreme and only love and to whom he is constantly faithful. It is the living Church, with a first name and a last name, which the priest shepherds in his parish or in the mission entrusted to him. That mission brings him joy whenever he is faithful to it, whenever he does all that he has to do and lets go of everything that he has to let go of, as long as he stands firm amid the flock that the Lord has entrusted to him: Feed my sheep (see John 21:16, 17).

Priestly joy is a joy that is sister to obedience. An obedience to the Church in the hierarchy that gives us, as it were, not simply the external framework for our obedience: the parish to which I am sent, my ministerial assignments, my particular work … but also union with God the Father, the source of all fatherhood. It is likewise an obedience to the Church in service: in availability and readiness to serve everyone, always, and as best I can, following the example of "Our Lady of Promptness" (see Luke 1:39, *meta spoudēs*), who hastens to serve Elizabeth her kinswoman and is concerned for the kitchen of Cana when the wine runs out. The availability of her priests makes the Church a house with open doors, a refuge for sinners, a home for people living on the streets, a place of loving care for the sick, a camp for the young, a classroom for catechizing children about to make their First Communion. . . . Wherever God's people have desires or needs, there is the priest, who knows how to listen (*ob-audire*) and feels a loving mandate from Christ, who sends him to relieve that need with mercy or to encourage those good desires with resourceful charity.

All who are called should know that genuine and complete joy does exist in this world: it is the joy of being taken from the people we love and then being sent back to them as dispensers of the gifts and counsels of Jesus, the one Good Shepherd who, with deep compassion for all the little ones and the outcasts of this earth, wearied and oppressed like sheep without a shepherd, wants to associate many others to his ministry, so as himself to remain with us and to work, in the person of his priests, for the good of his people.

On this Holy Thursday, I ask the Lord Jesus to enable many young people to discover that burning zeal that joy kindles in our hearts as soon as we have the stroke of boldness needed to respond willingly to his call.

On this Holy Thursday, I ask the Lord Jesus to preserve the joy sparkling in the eyes of the recently ordained who go forth to devour the world, to spend themselves fully in the midst of God's faithful people, rejoicing as they prepare their first homily, their first Mass, their first Baptism, their first Confession. . . . It is the joy of being able to share with wonder, and for the first time as God's anointed, the treasure of the Gospel and to feel the faithful people anointing you again and in yet another way: by their requests, by bowing their heads for your blessing, by taking your hands, by bringing you their children, by pleading for their sick. . . . Preserve, Lord, in your young priests the joy of going forth, of doing everything as if for the first time, the joy of spending their lives fully for you.

On this Thursday of the priesthood, I ask the Lord Jesus to confirm the priestly joy of those who have already ministered for some years. The joy which, without leaving their eyes, is also found on the shoulders of those who bear the burden of the ministry, those priests who, having experienced the labors of the apostolate, gather their strength and re-arm themselves: "get a second wind," as athletes would say. Lord, preserve the depth, wisdom, and maturity of the joy felt by these older priests. May they be able to pray with Nehemiah: "the joy of the Lord is my strength" (see Nehemiah 8:10).

Finally, on this Thursday of the priesthood, I ask the Lord Jesus to make better known the joy of elderly priests, whether healthy or infirm. It is the joy of the cross, which springs from the knowledge that we possess an imperishable treasure in perishable earthen vessels. May these priests find happiness wherever they are; may they experience already, in the passage of the years, a taste of eternity. May they know, Lord, the joy of handing on the torch, the joy of seeing new generations of their spiritual children, and of hailing the promises from afar, smiling and at peace, in that hope which does not disappoint.

The Oil of Gladness

THE FRAMEWORK AND CENTER of this Chrism liturgy is gladness, or joy. The Lord came to proclaim a Year of Grace, a Holy Year, a Jubilee Year. Although in its roots it refers to a musical instrument, *jubilatio* is the Latin word used to describe "peasants' shouts of joy," the joy of humble laborers, of those with little power. *Jubilare* is "to shout excitedly with joy like the humble and the poor when they sing. To burst forth in shouts of praise to God." This is what Isaiah describes in the first reading: the promised Lord who will come to bind the broken hearts and transform the dejection of the humble into "songs" of joy.

Joy is the joy of the powerless, of the workers who "reap with shouts of joy what they sowed with tears"; of the shepherds to whom the angels proclaimed on Christmas night; of Our Lady. Joy is the joy of Mary and Elizabeth, that joy that filled their souls and makes them overflow with a contagious joy; it is the joy of Jesus: Saint Luke tells us that the Lord was filled with joy in the Holy Spirit, and he praised his Father because he had revealed these things to children. And if we look closely, the joy of the humble is the joy that is, in turn, given to work: at the harvest, at the beginning of the mission, and at the end of it. It is the joy that comes after suffering something for Christ, as happened to the apostles who went out and "rejoiced that they were worthy to suffer dishonor for the sake of his name" (Acts 5:41). It is the singing that is unleashed after being constrained by the anxieties of work. Singing unites and strengthens: "Do not be grieved, for the joy of the Lord is your strength" (Nehemiah 8:10).

Today we would do well to ask ourselves, as priests and priestly people: What brings joy to our heart? This is no marginal question, no question in a minor key. To ask ourselves if there is joy in our heart—to give thanks for it and to ask for it—is to wonder about what unites us in holiness and makes our pastoral work effective, to wonder about our humility and strength.

The Chrism Mass is a Mass of joy for priests: from the joy of unity. It is the same Lord who is sending each of us on mission and has dispersed us throughout the archdiocese and even beyond, who brings us together on Holy Thursday, who places the Eucharist in the chalice and makes us feel united in his hands so we can be shared again and again in the midst of God's faithful people. All joy comes from this priestly communion, which is a gift from Jesus our Lord: union in the Holy Spirit and union with the spouse, which is the Church, one and holy. From this attitude all the joyful attitudes of the priestly heart spring up.

Pope John Paul II points out the framework for the great joys that will fill our heart this Holy Year: the joy of the pilgrimage guiding the faithful people of God toward the Father's house; the joy of crossing thresholds and passing through the door, which is Christ; the joy of having a purified memory because we asked for pardon; the profound joy that is the fruit of heroic charity; and the dramatic joy that seizes the memory when we remember our martyrs. And, along with these big joys, if one can say that, are the small joys that are part of the everyday life of the priestly heart.

In Gospel terms, we can affirm without fear that a strong priestly heart is one that is able, for example, to jump for joy watching his catechists give classes to children, or youth go out at night to look after the homeless. A priestly heart is strong if it is always able to jump for joy at the return of the prodigal son who was waiting patiently in the confessional. A priestly heart is strong if it is able to let the joy keep burning within at the words of the unrecognized Jesus, who becomes our companion along the way, as happened to the disciples going to Emmaus. Let us not forget: the joy of the Lord is our strength; it protects us against the spirit of complaint, which signals a lack of hope, and against all impatience, more typical of bureaucrats than of priestly hearts.

Joy, humility, and strength go together closely; they are the graces that we, together with our faithful people, ask the Lord to give us priests on this Holy Thursday of the Jubilee Year. To receive the joy that comes from the Holy Spirit, we ask Our Lady to teach us how it is that the greatest are the most humble. To receive the grace of humility, we ask the servant that she teach us what it is to sing the Magnificat in daily humble service and fraternal encounter. To receive the grace of strength we ask the Blessed Virgin to teach us what it is never to separate joy and humility but always to keep them united, and we ask her that arrogance never separate our hearts from the friends of her son Jesus, but that we love and accept ourselves humbly as brothers so that "the joy of the Lord may be our strength."

The Importance of Anointing

THE IMAGE OF JESUS anointed and consecrated to anoint his people, beginning with those most in need, fills us with hope and shows us the way in this time of deep crisis in our life as a nation. The Father anoints his Son with an anointing that makes him a man "for" others. He anoints him to send him to proclaim the Good News, to cure, to set free. Thus there is nothing in the Son that does not come from the Father, nor is there anything in him that is not "for" us. Jesus is anointed to anoint. And we, his priests, are also anointed to anoint.

In the Gospel scene in Luke 4:16–30, there is something special that draws our attention: Jesus reads from Isaiah, sits down and proclaims with anointing and simple majesty: "Today this scripture has been fulfilled in your hearing." Although the Lord had already been teaching in the synagogues (Luke 4:15) and his fame had spread throughout the region, it is evident that he has only recently begun his mission. Thus, how is it possible to speak of fulfillment? This way of speaking shocked his countrymen and challenged them: "Do here also in your hometown the things that we have heard you did at Capernaum" (Luke 4:23). It's like saying to him, you have to keep proving with new miracles that you are the anointed one. This demand for more signs will be a constant in those who refuse to believe in Jesus.

Our attention is also drawn to the fact that Jesus speaks of fulfillment when he has barely begun his mission. Does this dispirited phrase not resonate within us at times: why don't you perform here and now those miracles that we have heard that you did then? This phrase separates us from the style of the Anointed One: in Jesus the promises are fulfilled every day, and when we do not notice or succeed in seeing it, the Gospel phrase should rather be: "I believe, Lord, but increase my faith!"

The same thing that happens with the Eucharist that is renewed every day with the poverty of bread also happens with the health and freedom that the Lord gives us. We can say that all of the Anointed One's gestures—his words of proclamation, his acts of healing, the vision he communicates to us, and the freedom he gives us—are characterized by poverty. Poor are his gestures and actions: they are for today; and although his anointing was "once and for all," it needs constant renewal and refreshment, a continual rooting in the poverty of every moment of our history.

This is how Jesus proceeds. For him, to cure a sick person is not only to cure him of his particular sickness but to anoint him so that he is changed, with his pain anointed, into a witness to the love of God and connected to Jesus' saving Passion. Jesus gives sight to the blind but not just so they can see their own interests for themselves without the help of others. For him, to give sight is to anoint the eyes so that faith bursts forth and the practice of charity is strengthened thanks to the joy that allows one "to see what cannot be seen," to see with hope. For Jesus, to set the oppressed free does not free one of all burden so he or she can race through life alone making a career. To set free from all slavery is to anoint so that the anointed burden becomes the saving weight of the cross, and so that, freed from all oppression, we can carry our cross with a positive spirit, and following the Lord, help others to carry theirs.

What I mean is that the anointing falls not so much on "things" but on the most intimate part of the person, where it abounds to overflowing. The depth and efficacy of the Lord's anointing are not measured by the quantity of miracles that can be performed, nor by how far he gets in his mission nor by the depth of his suffering. The depth, which reaches to the marrow of his bones, and the efficacy that allows all of him to be salvation for the one who draws near to him are rooted in his intimate union and total identification with the Father who sent him. It is precisely this anointing with which Jesus lives his union with the Father that makes his every gesture a fulfillment. Anointing is what transforms his time into *kairos*, into a time of permanent grace.

The mission is fulfilled "today" because the Lord not only gives bread but he himself becomes bread. This release that he gives to the oppressed is fulfilled "today" because the Lord not only forgives by "removing stains" from outer garments but he himself "becomes sin"; he gets dirty, is left with wounds, and so he puts himself in the hands of the Father who accepts him. This good news is fulfilled "today" because the Lord not only announces what measures he is going to take, but he himself is the measure that makes us see with the light that his every word holds. We, too, dear brothers in the priesthood, are anointed to anoint. Anointed, that is to say, anointed from the marrow of our bones with Jesus and with the Father. As in Baptism, priestly anointing acts from the inside out. The opposite to what it appears, the priesthood is not a grace that comes from the outside and never succeeds in entering into the depths of our sinful souls. We are priests in the most intimate, sacred, and mysterious part of our heart, right there where we are children by Baptism and the indwelling of the Trinity. Our moral effort consists in anointing, with that most profound anointing, our daily and more exterior gestures in a way that our life becomes, through our collaboration, what we already are by grace.

Anointed to anoint, that is to say, to incorporate every person into this union with the Father and the Son in the same Spirit. May our priestly anointing keep changing us into bread as we anoint daily bread by consecrating it in every Eucharist and by sharing it in solidarity with our brothers and sisters. May our priestly anointing keep changing us into men full of tenderness as we anoint with balm the pain of those who are sick. May our priestly anointing free us from our sins as we anoint the sins of our brothers and sisters with the Spirit of forgiveness and help them to carry their crosses. May our priestly anointing keep changing us into light for the world as we preach the Gospel by anointing, as the Lord ordered, teaching obedience to all that he commanded us. May our priestly anointing anoint our time, and the use we make of it, so that it becomes a "time of grace" for our brothers and sisters, as we follow, to the ecclesial rhythm of the breviary, the ordinary course of life that the Lord gives us.

We are living in a climate where credibility is in short supply, and in which every public person must check daily that what happened to Jesus' compatriots is not happening to us. May we not seek or claim credibility other than that which comes from the anointing of Christ. As John says, "As for you, the anointing that you received from him abides in you, and so you do not need anyone to teach you. . . . His anointing teaches you all about things, and is true and is not just a lie" (1 John 2:27). Only those who live and become by anointing are worthy of faith. May Mary, who was the first fully to experience the presence of the Anointed One within, transmit to us the joy of her hope-filled vision, and with heavenly tenderness open to us the sphere in which, through our hands, the anointing of God passes to his faithful people.

The Perfect Gift

"TODAY THIS SCRIPTURE has been fulfilled in your hearing." We know what followed: that there was a homily that was well participated in, with exclamations of admiration from the people and ironic phrases, like the one about the son of the carpenter; and that Jesus provoked his countrymen with those very emphatic affirmations about the prophet's lack of acceptance in his own country and about the miracles that God couldn't do in their town because of their lack of faith. We know that tempers flared to the point of wanting to hurl Jesus off the cliff, but that at the height of their exasperation the Lord passed through the midst of them and went to Capernaum to preach.

The opening of the year of the Lord's favor proved very disconcerting. Mind you, the image that remains is one of liturgical majesty, with the Lord dominating the scene. He gets up to do a reading and the episode concludes when "he passed through the midst of them and went on his way." Although the liturgy finished outside the synagogue, the ending is like one of our exits from Mass through the midst of the people.

It's as if what occurred during the Lord's entire public life had been advanced and concentrated in a short period of time: the evangelization of the poor, the miracles, the people's approval, then indignation and leading him to the cross, and the Lordship of the risen Jesus. The Lord makes the proclamation and causes things to flare up, but he doesn't allow them to do away

61

with him right now. This is the prophetic opening of the year of favor. With his words and gestures, and with what he permitted the others to say and do, the Lord dramatically begins his mission for which he was anointed.

The Lord had his countrymen go from wonder to rejection. Why, we may ask. First, they are all speaking well of him and were amazed at the gracious words that came from his lips. But minutes later they wanted to throw him over a cliff. Did he have to provoke the people? Didn't the Anointed One come to bring Good News to the poor, to announce the year of the Lord's favor? Why did he confuse them? Wouldn't Our Lady, who was surely present, have remembered the words of Simeon: "This child is destined for the falling and the rising of many in Israel, and to be a sign that will be opposed so that the thoughts of many will be revealed—and a sword will piece your own soul too" (Luke 2:34–35).

The goodness with which Jesus was anointed is a "today" so strong and has a power of fulfillment so intense that it produces opposition and that pays little attention to good manners; it makes what everyone has in his heart come out. To some, such as Our Lady, Jesus' presence opens their souls as with a sword, and anoints them with his Spirit, pouring out all his love on them. To others, such as the Pharisees, it does not allow them to hide their selfishness or lay aside their anger, and makes them stubborn in their closed-mindedness. The today of the Anointed One questions, uncovers, disconnects positions taken. The Lord proclaims the Good News that frees and makes one see. Here is where some people let themselves be anointed and tasked with helping others, while others close their eyes and return to their servitude where they feel more comfortable and secure.

Thus we see that the mission of love for which the Lord is anointed by the Spirit cannot be accomplished without first pulling the plug on selfishness. The Lord comes to proclaim the Good News that faith was waiting for, and that unplugs us by making us expose our skepticism (that which always thinks, "is not this Joseph's son?") so that we can devote our whole faith to him; the Lord comes to provide the service of mercy that frees us from our sin and puts before us the option of being like the widows or lepers of Israel who were left uncared for, or like Naaman the Syrian or Zarephath's widow who was looked after. The Lord comes to inaugurate his Kingdom, and with his humility and meekness frees us from all comfortable dreams of power and ecclesiastical vanity and invites us to make ourselves available to serve others.

The word and the gestures of the Lord free and open the eyes of all. Nobody remains indifferent. One is either changed and asks for help and light or remains closed and clings even harder to his chains and darkness.

The mission that the Lord carries out is not an external thing—I proclaim and later you see; it is a mission that for him implies the total gift of self, and for those who receive him it implies receiving him in his entirety. Then comes the anointing. The anointing is a total gift. Only those who have the anointing can be anointed, and to be anointed they have to forsake and lose themselves to receive this total gift. Jesus, the beloved Son, is the Anointed One because he received everything from the Father. The Lord has nothing for himself nor does anything for himself: in him all is anointing received and fulfillment of mission. Just as he receives everything, he gives everything, through service and the surrender of his life on the cross. To be able to receive so total a gift we need the Lord to teach us to forsake ourselves, to humble ourselves, to lose ourselves.

Faith, for example, is anointing with trust and total adherence, and thus one needs to be stripped of his intellectual reservations and preconceptions. The faithful people turned to the Lord with this faith, offered all their trust, and thus the Lord was able to anoint them with healing. Charity is also an anointing—it is to anoint the other with our works of mercy but performed from the gift of our very selves, which supposes forsaking and surrendering: charity anoints the other with the total gift of self not with the gift of things. And the Lord "uninstalls" us to be able to anoint us.

The Spirit anoints the Lord today to carry out his mission today, in this permanent today of the Kingdom. The anointing is so total that it is always today; when it is received everything is transformed into today. Faith is today, hope is today, charity is today, here and now. There is no room to put anything into parentheses. Thus, the Lord needs to free us from what prevents us from being anointed today to anoint others. Anointing seals a today that becomes permanent, that becomes Church, assembly. Anointing seals a mission that requires the whole person, every day, to go everywhere wholeheartedly to anoint all men and women. That is why anointing is truly catholic, both quantitatively and qualitatively.

The Lord's short homily was an act of love, not bravado. Only a word of love can free the other so that he or she is open to anointing. If some reacted with hatred, it is because it was inside of them. The loving word of Jesus revealed this, and they could have repented instead of hardening in this attitude. That God always frees us is an act of love. Jesus is saying to his people that, in this moment, a much greater miracle is being performed than the ones at Capernaum: the holy year is beginning, the year of the Anointed One who comes to anoint with the Spirit, the time of grace. The invitation is so strong that it overwhelms his countrymen, and they don't know what to do with him. They couldn't even stone him. Jesus launches the Kingdom showing himself sovereign. Thus, detached from everything—including his countrymen's favorable opinion—he begins to preach and make the Kingdom real.

Jesus' first homily, which in Luke inaugurates the mission in the Temple environs, was and continued to be dramatically destabilizing. Jesus frees us from any attitude other than keeping our eyes fixed on him. "The eyes of all in the synagogue were fixed on him," the faithful witness. The Letter to the Hebrews expresses this beautifully: "Since we are surrounded by so great a cloud of witnesses, let us also lay aside every weight and the sin that clings so closely, and let us run with perseverance the race that is set before us, looking to Jesus, the pioneer and perfecter of our faith, who for the sake of the joy that was set before him endured the cross, disregarding its shame, and has taken his seat at the right hand of the throne of God" (Hebrews 12:1–2).

We ask the Lord, then, for this grace: That detached from sin we may run the race that is proposed to us with our eyes fixed on Jesus. Just as he was detached from the joy that was being proposed to him to come to find us, his prodigal children, his lost sheep.

That today of Jesus detaches us from all pasts in which, sometimes out of stubbornness and at others out of comfort, we seek refuge, and from all futures that, sometimes out of ambition and at others out of fear, we try to control and situate ourselves in, the today of the love of God, this love which, as the Pope says, "is indeed 'ecstasy,' not in the sense of a moment of intoxication, but rather as a journey, an ongoing exodus out of the closed inward-looking self towards its liberation through self-giving, and thus towards authentic self-discovery and indeed the discovery of God: 'Whoever seeks to gain his life will lose it, but whoever loses his life will preserve it' (Luke 17:33)" (*Deus caritas est*, 6).

The "Today" of Jesus

THE "TODAY" OF JESUS impresses me, that today so unique in which the millenary and patient hope of the people of Israel is focused on the Anointed One and extended again into the time of charity and of the Church's Gospel proclamation.

Today we ask the Lord for the grace to care like him for the fragility of our people; last year we asked to go out to find our people with apostolic audacity. I would like us to stop for a few moments to experience how this fragility and this audacity are embedded in the "today" of Jesus. That "today" of Jesus is *kairos*, a time of grace, source of Living Water and Light, that wells up from the eternal Word made flesh—flesh with history, with culture, with time.

The Church lives in the today of Jesus, and this Chrism Mass, prelude to Easter, that brings us together as a single priestly body in this holy space of our cathedral, is one of the fullest expressions of the today of Jesus, this perennial today of the Last Supper, source of forgiveness, communion, and service. He is with us proclaiming his Word, freeing us from our enslavements, binding our wounded hearts. Only in the today of Jesus is the fragility of our faithful people well cared for. Only in the today of Jesus is apostolic audacity efficacious and fruitful.

Outside of this today—outside the time of the Kingdom, the time of grace, of glad tidings, of freedom and of mercy—the other times, the political, economic and technological times, tend to become times that devour us, exclude us, oppress us. When these human times cease to be in tune and in tension with God's time they become foreign: repetitive, parallel, too short, or infinitely long. They become inhuman times: economics ignores hunger or the lack of a school for children or the miserable situation of the elderly; technological time is so instantaneous and laden with images that it does not let the hearts and minds of youth mature; political time seems to be circular at times, like that of a merry-go-round in which the ring is always the same. However, the today of Jesus, which at first sight can seem boring and a little unexciting, is a time in which treasures of wisdom and charity are hidden, a time rich in love, rich in faith, and very rich in hope.

The today of Jesus is a time with memory: memory of the family, memory of the people, memory of the Church in which the memory of all the saints is alive.

The liturgy is the expression of this ever-living memory. The today of Jesus is a time laden with hope, future, and heaven, of which we already have a deposit, and we are living it in advance with every consolation that the Lord gives us. The today of Jesus is a time in which the present is a constant call and renewed invitation to the concrete charity of daily service to the poorest person, who fills our heart with joy. In this today we want to go out to meet our people, every day.

In the today of Jesus fear of conflict or uncertainty or anxiety has no place. There is no place for fear of conflict because in the today of the Lord "perfect love casts out fear." There is no place for uncertainty because the Lord is with us always "to the end of the age"; he has promised this, and we know "in whom we have put our trust." There is no place for anxiety because the today of Jesus is the today of the Father who "knows what we need" and in whose hands we feel that "today's trouble is enough for today." There is no place for uneasiness because the Spirit will make us say and do what is needed at the right time.

The audacity of the Lord is not limited to occasional or extraordinary gestures. It is an apostolic audacity that is shaped, we might say, by each fragility, each fragile moment. And this fragility leads it into God's time. This today of Jesus creates the space and sets the time for this encounter. To set out to encounter the fragility of our people, we must first enter that time of the Lord's grace. First, in prayer, our hearts need to be strengthened to feel that they are experiencing the fulfillment of the promises. Then we can set forth with audacity, trusting in providence, truly open to others, without the blinkers of self-interest but with eagerness for the interests of the Lord.

But there is also another way to enter into the Lord's time. This consists in going out of ourselves and entering into the time of our faithful people. Our faithful people live this today of Jesus much more than you might at times think. And it greatly helps our spiritual fervor and trust in God that, as pastors, we let our hearts be shaped in the midst of our people's fragilities and by the way they bear them. To let the heart be shaped is to know how to read, for example, in the humble and insistent claims of our people the witness of a faith able to focus their whole experience of God's love for them into a simple gesture of receiving a blessing (how beautiful that our faithful people know how to be thankful for a blessing!). To let the heart be shaped is to know how to read in the long time between our people's confessions the rhythm of the pilgrim life, of the long term, marked by big celebrations . . . to know how to read, say, a hope that maintains the thread of God's love unscathed throughout the year, and that helps them cope with life's highs and lows. The proclamation of the angel is always present in the heart of our people: "Do not be afraid; for see—I am bringing you good news of great joy for all the people: to you is born this day in the city of David a Savior, who is the Messiah, the Lord" (Luke 2:10–11). This today of Jesus who is born in the midst of the people is the today of the Father who says to him: "You are my Son, today I have begotten you" (see Hebrews 5:1–6).

Let us enter the saving today of Jesus, who says to us: "Today this scripture has been fulfilled in your hearing." Let us enter the today of our faithful people. Feeling united with Jesus, the Good Shepherd, let us go out to meet our people. To look after their hope, with Jesus, with the glad tidings of the Gospel every day. To look after their charity, with Jesus, releasing captives and the oppressed. To look after their faith, with Jesus, restoring sight to the blind.

Let us ask Saint Joseph, whose feast was celebrated at the beginning of Holy Week, to make us enter, actively and contemplatively, into the today of Jesus, the adopted son whom he helped to raise. Saint Joseph was graced to enter first into this today of Jesus in which Mary had already entered and to see the child continue to grow in stature, wisdom, and grace. Saint Joseph knew how to care for the fragilities—those of Mary and the child—that ended up strengthening his own. May he grant us this grace.

The Grace of Unity

*If then there is any encouragement in Christ, any consola-
tion from love, any sharing in the Spirit, any compassion
and sympathy, make my joy complete: be of the same mind,
having the same love, being in full accord and of one mind.
Do nothing from selfish ambition or conceit, but in humility regard others as better than yourselves. Let each of you
look not to your own interests, but to the interests of others.
(Philippians 2:1–4)*

*He said also to the one who had invited him, "When you
give a luncheon or a dinner, do not invite your friends or
your brothers or your relatives or rich neighbors, in case they
may invite you in return, and you would be repaid. But
when you give a banquet, invite the poor, the crippled, the
lame, and the blind. And you will be blessed, because they
cannot repay you, for you will be repaid at the resurrection of
the righteous." (Luke 14:12–14)*

THE TONE with which the Apostle speaks to the Christian
community is moving: the name of Christ, the consolation from love, the sharing in the spirit, the tenderness and
compassion . . . a tone that forms the framework for the dialogue between the pastor and his people (Philippians 2:1). A

language that arises from the very bowels of the pastor in whom the answer of the people will make his joy complete. How many times has the Lord, out of his pure grace, permitted us to have this experience! Experience forged in the silence of prayer, in trusting abandonment, in the call of Jesus Christ (that certainty of knowing in whom we have put our trust), in the patient listening of the brothers and sisters committed to our care, in tribulation and the cross, in the firm hope of final contemplation of the wonderful face of Jesus Christ.

So, the dialogue between the pastor and the people is framed in this way and moves toward achieving what Paul expresses: the unity of the Church, "being in full accord" (Philippians 2:2) so that everyone is united. He is bold in his letters: "Love one another with mutual affection; outdo one another in showing honor" (Romans 12:10). "Live in harmony with one another; do not be haughty, but associate with the lowly" (Romans 12:16). And, on various occasions, he speaks of begetting, bearing, giving birth (see 1 Corinthians 4:14; Galatians 4:19), that is to say, continuing to give life and unity to the people of God, preserving the unity of the people from whom he was taken, of whom he was a part, and to whom he was sent. And the unity was woven daily with the directives that he himself issued: have the same love, be in full accord, do nothing from selfish ambition or conceit, in humility regard others as better than yourselves, don't look to your own interests, but to the interests of others (see Philippians 2:3–4). Here is seen the mettle of the pastor who wearily desires and fine-tunes the unity guarded by these parameters that shape a defined spiritual space.

Moreover, in the Gospel passage we just read there are instructions from the Lord that, in some way, point to this pastoral space, the only one suitable to bring about the unity of the faithful people of God and ourselves: "And when you give a banquet, invite the poor, the crippled, the lame, and the blind" (Luke 14:12–14). This is the spiritual realm sought by selflessness to the point of self-emptying. Jesus reminds us of the subtle deception that exists in doing something for our own benefit and receiving a reward; he indicates for us at the same time that there is a sure place where the selfishness that nests in our heart cannot trick us: "neighbor empathy" and welcoming those who cannot reward us. Once again this oft-repeated leitmotif of the Anointed One's mission implicitly appears (see Luke 4:18–19).

The pastor brings about and molds this unity of his people from the self-emptying of himself in the daily provision of service, seeking out the interests of Christ Jesus and not his own. The unity of the Church is a grace, pure grace, but a grace that we have to know how to receive, desiring it intimately, making space for it, making our heart increasingly hollow by emptying it of all worldly interests. Thus, in the first reading, Saint Paul explains to us the contours of these spaces of receptivity to grace that I just referred to: the same love, the same mind, no selfish ambition or conceit, regarding others as better than yourselves. And, to alleviate all doubt, the Gospel brings us the image of those who cannot repay to highlight the profound gratuitousness of the feast.

And because it is about gratuitousness, the true unity of the Church, true unity among us, is obtained only gratis, as pure gift of the Lord; may we always be ready to receive it, walking the path he has set. The first reading is precisely the introduction that presents this to us: though he was in the form of God . . . taking the form of a slave . . . he humbled himself and became obedient (see Philippians 2:6–11). And Paul stresses, "Let the same mind be in you that was in Christ Jesus" (Philippians 2:5).

This is the path to follow; this is the theological place to receive the grace of unity. That is the existential cavity that makes us capable of such grace. This is the desire that is opening the necessary space in our hearts. Self-emptying becomes service, and from there the unity of the Church is molded; there the Spirit can work. Only from there can we be receivers and makers of unity, that is to say, by leaving it to the Holy Spirit to create unity and shape the harmony of the Church. As the Church Fathers used to say, "*Ipse harmonia est*—the Holy Spirit is harmony itself."

Let us ask the Lord to infect us with this attitude of self-emptying service that never seeks its own interests. The same attitude that Our Mother, as the first disciple, assumed. The attitude that will give us paternal "tenderness" and brotherly "compassion" to exhort our people and ourselves to make our joy complete by "being in full accord" (Philippians 2:2). Amen.

The Lively Dialogue
That Is Preaching

In considering the Sunday Eucharist more than thirty years after the Council, we need to assess how well the word of God is being proclaimed and how effectively the People of God have grown in knowledge and love of Sacred Scripture (Dies Domini, 40).

THESE WORDS from Saint John Paul II are the inspiration for these simple reflections about the Sunday homily. The Pope tightly links a question—How are we proclaiming the Word, how are we preaching?—to a work of reflection: to verify the real, effective growth of knowledge and love for the Sacred Scriptures among the People of God. This love that, coupled with knowledge, translates into "lived experience," and complements the "celebratory" aspect of the Eucharist.

We do well to link these things. If we want to know how we are preaching, we should always check on our faithful people's knowledge and love of the Word. It was precisely with the word that our Lord won the hearts of the people. They came from everywhere to hear him (Mark 1:45). They were astounded at his teachings (Mark 6:2). They felt he spoke as one who had authority (Mark 1:27). It was with the word that the apostles, those he appointed "to be with him and to be sent out to proclaim the message" (Mark 3:14), attracted the nations to the bosom of the Church (see Mark 16:15–20).

The Homily as Planting and Harvesting

But what does it mean "to verify"? Clearly this knowledge and love are not verified by looking at statistics that count only how many go to Sunday Mass or buy Bibles. Rather, verification has to come from the look of a good sower.

A sower's look is confident and long term. The sower doesn't spy daily on what he has planted; whether he is asleep or awake, he knows that the seed grows by itself.

A sower's look is hopeful. The sower, when he sees weeds growing up in the middle of the wheat, does not react with complaints and alarm. He bets on the fruitfulness of the seed against the temptation to rush time.

A sower's look is loving on those who realize that charity's fecundity is freely given; although the seed seems to be wasted in many fields, where it bears fruit it does so superabundantly.

From this look will spring a homily that both plants and harvests. Whether the preacher prepares his preaching or dialogues with the people, the Spirit will put on his lips words that sow and reap. Feeling and pondering in his heart the knowledge and love of the people for the Word, the preacher prays for a valuable harvest that is mature; he shows how to implement it, and he plants a desire, one more hope, where the soil is good and suitable for seed to grow.

The Delightful and Comforting Joy of Preaching

As pastors, it is up to each of us to preach at our Masses, and every day, every Sunday, it does us good to renew our fervor for preparing the homily, first verifying if our own knowledge and love of the Word that we preach are growing. As Paul says, "We speak, not to please mortals, but to please God who tests our hearts" (1 Thessalonians 2:4).

If our love for first listening to the Word that we have to preach is alive, as is our love for receiving the Eucharist that we consecrate, it will be transmitted in one way or another to the faithful people of God. In *Evangelii nuntiandi*, Pope Paul VI spoke to us of "the delightful and comforting joy of evangelizing."

> God . . . wishes the seed to bear fruit through the voice of the ministers of the Gospel; and it will depend on us whether this grows into trees and produces its full fruit. Let us therefore preserve our fervor of spirit. Let us preserve the delightful and comforting joy of evangelizing, even when it is in tears that we must sow (Evangelii nuntiandi, 80).

This reflection points to that rule of all good homilies that says, "it is from the abundance of the heart that the mouth speaks." The Sunday readings will resonate gloriously in the people's hearts if they first resonated in the pastor's heart.

"Do All That He Commands You"

For this, the image of Our Lady can help. She is the one who best transmits to the faithful people the joy of this Word that first filled her with joy. That's why the Pope, at the end of his apostolic letter, puts forth Our Lady as the model to which the faithful, including the preacher, look:

> As they listen to the word proclaimed in the Sunday assembly, the faithful look to the Virgin Mary, learning from her to keep it and ponder it in their hearts (cf. Luke 2:19) (Dies Domini, 86).

We, too, can put this image at the beginning of our reflection and tell ourselves that a good Sunday homily should have the flavor of that new wine that renews both the preacher's heart and the listeners' hearts. And in this new wine, Mary is the expert from Cana. The grace to say to the faithful with Mary (with her maternal tone), "Do whatever he tells you," is the grace that we should ask for in every homily. Our Lady's maternal tone is that of the "Believer in the Word" and of the "Servant of the Word."

> *The priest ought to be the first "believer" in the word, while being fully aware that the words of his ministry are not "his," but those of the One who sent him. He is not the master of the word, but its servant. He is not the sole possessor of the word; in its regard he is in debt to the People of God. Precisely because he can and does evangelize, the priest—like every other member of the Church—ought to grow in awareness that he himself is continually in need of being evangelized (Pastores dabo vobis, 26).*

The Homily as a Dialogue between God and His People

> *It should also be borne in mind that the liturgical proclamation of the word of God, especially in the Eucharistic assembly, is not so much a time for meditation and catechesis as a dialogue between God and his People, a dialogue in which the wonders of salvation are proclaimed and the demands of the Covenant are continually restated (Dies Domini, 40).*

That the homily is less a moment of meditation and catechesis than "the lively dialogue between God and man" is an evaluation of the preaching that comes from its being integrated in the Eucharist. It supposes catechesis and is in continuity with it, but it goes beyond to be the highest moment of dialogue between God and his people, before sacramental communion. The Lord is truly pleased to dialogue with his people and with us who, by our preaching, make the people sense the Lord's joy.

The homily, then, is a taking-up again of this dialogue that is already established between the Lord and his people. That's why the preacher has to sound out and evaluate the heart of the community in order to dialogue with this heart, seeking out where the desire for God is alive and ardent, and also where that dialogue, which began as a loving one, was "robbed" or "suffocated" or failed to bear fruit.

In the Puebla documents there is a beautiful paragraph that sheds light for us on the identity of the people with whom the Lord is pleased to dialogue. The people of Latin America are a people on whose soul "the faith of the Church has set its seal" (*Puebla,* 445). That's why it is infallible in believing [*infallibilitas in credendo*] in the sense of *Lumen gentium* (12). It is a wise people for whom "this wisdom is also a principle of discernment and an evangelical instinct through which they spontaneously sense when the Gospel is served in the Church and when it is emptied of its content and stifled by other interests" (*Puebla,* 448; see also John Paul II, Opening Address, III.6).

The bishops pick up on the Pope's phrase in the opening speech. I think it is the key to becoming conscious of the mystery of love that reigns between God and his faithful people, and to knowing with whom we are speaking. This "faith instinct" that makes our people infallible in believing should be the heartfelt criterion by which we orient our preaching.

The people's religious life is not just an object of evangelization. Insofar as it is a concrete embodiment of the Word of God, it is itself an active way in which the people continually evangelize themselves (Puebla, 450).

What does it mean to preach to those who are continually evangelizing themselves and are infallible in believing? Dropping the vain discussion of how much there still is to "explain" to the people of God, I think that the image of a mother and child best clarifies what it means to have to teach those who already know. The Church is the mother, and she preaches to the people like a mother speaks to her child, confident that the child already knows that all that is taught will be for the better because he knows he is loved. Parents know how to be guided by this innate sense in children, which gives them the measure of when they overstepped a boundary or said something inappropriate. It is the spirit of love that reigns in a family that guides both the mother and the child in their dialogues, in which the child is taught and learns, is valued and corrected. And so it is with the homily: this learning in the spirit of the family is what guides the speaker and the listener. The Spirit who inspired the Gospels also inspires how they are to be preached and how they are to be heard in every Eucharist.

This mother–church context, in which the dialogue between the Lord and his people develops, should be encouraged and cultivated by the preacher's friendly closeness, the warmth of our tone of voice, the gentle style of our phrases, the joy of our gestures. If this maternal-church spirit is present, even what some may find boring on occasion can be fruitful in the long run, just as a mother's "boring advice" bears fruit in time in her children's hearts.

One can only be amazed at the resources that the Lord had to talk to his people, to convey full revelation to all, to captivate common people with difficult, demanding teachings. I believe that the secret to Jesus' appeal is hidden in the ecclesial context that the Spirit establishes among those who worship the Father. Jesus' conviction is expressed in this: "Do not be afraid, little flock, for it is your Father's good pleasure to give you the king-dom" (Luke 12:32). Jesus preaches in this Spirit. That's why, full of joy in the Spirit, he blesses the Father, who draws the little ones to himself:

> *At that hour Jesus rejoiced in the Holy Spirit and said, "I thank you, Father, Lord of heaven and earth, because you have hidden these things from the wise and intelligent and have revealed them to infants; yes, Father, for such was your gracious will. All things have been handed over to me by my Father; and no one knows who the Son is except the Father, or who the Father is except the Son and anyone to whom the Son chooses to reveal him" (Luke 10:21–22).*

Beyond the resources that in the Gospel are infinite in quan-tity and quality the preacher has the most beautiful and diffi-cult mission of uniting the hearts that love each other—the Lord's and the people's—hearts that remain silent during the homily and let him speak. Both the Lord and his people speak to each other in a thousand ways directly and without inter-mediaries. But during the homily they want someone to be the mediator and to express the feelings of both, in such a way that, afterward, each chooses where to continue the conversation. The Word is fundamentally mediating and requires not only the two who converse but also a mediator who represents it as such, a mediator who, like Paul, is convinced that "we do not proclaim ourselves; we proclaim Jesus Christ as Lord and our-selves as your slaves for Jesus' sake" (2 Corinthians 4:4).

A dialogue is much more than the communication of a truth. Dialogue is realized through the joy of talking and for the concrete good that is communicated with words between those who love each other. This good does not consist of things but of persons who give themselves mutually to one another in the dialogue. That's why purely moralistic, exegetical preaching reduces the communication between hearts that should happen in the homily and that should have a quasi-sacramental nature because "faith comes from what is heard, and what is heard comes through the word of Christ" (Romans 10:17).

"The Wonders of Salvation and the Demands of the Covenant" in the Homily

> . . . *a dialogue in which the wonders of salvation are proclaimed and the demands of the Covenant are continually restated (Dies Domini, 41).*

Dialogue is the proclamation of the wonders of salvation, in which the glory of God and of man alive shine. The dialogue between God and his people strengthens the covenant between them and tightens the bonds of charity. That's why it is key that in the homily truth goes hand in hand with beauty and goodness. It is not a question of cold, abstract truths, much less if delivered in handfuls and syllogisms. The homily requires that in the proclamation of every Gospel truth we know how to discover and communicate the beauty of the images the Lord uses to attract the attention (the parables are the most beautiful example) and, I would say, the opportunity—the *kairos*—that his love discovered or created to encourage the practice of good.

The memory of the faithful, like that of Mary, must be brimming with the wonders of God, and their hearts hopeful in the joyful, enabling practice of the love communicated to them. And this is so because every Word in the Scriptures is first gift rather than requirement.

The Deposit of Faith within the Faithful in the Homily

This synthesis of truth, beauty, and goodness is not something that needs to be invented: it is inherent in the Word incarnate, and where this Word has been received by a people and incorporated in their culture, the synthesis is what we call "popular religiosity."

> *At its core the religiosity of the people is a storehouse of values that offers the answers of Christian wisdom to the great questions of life (Puebla, 449).*

In this statement from Puebla we encounter beauty as "admiration before the great questions of existence." I say admiration because the answer is usually embodied in rituals, art, and popular celebrations. We encounter truth as "Christian wisdom" and goodness as "wealth of values." The love of God creates a people; it always creates a culture because it is binding in a stable, faithful way, and it engenders ways of seeing, feeling, and creating commonalities among human beings.

Christian preaching, therefore, encounters in the cultural heart of our people a source of living water for what has to be said and for how it has to be said. Just as we all prefer to be spoken to in our mother tongue—and even more if we have to use other languages—so also in the faith we like to be spoken to in the codes of our "mother culture." Of course, from there we grow, open up, and improve. When we are spoken to in our mother tongue, our heart is disposed to listen better. This language has a tone that conveys *parrhesia*, like that of the mother of the Maccabee sons, and also a synthesis achieved, a wisdom in which one feels at home. As Puebla says,

> *The Catholic wisdom of the common people is capable of fashioning a vital synthesis. It creatively combines the divine and*

the human, Christ and Mary, spirit and body, communion and institution, person and community, faith and home-land, intelligence and emotion. This wisdom is a Christian humanism that radically affirms the dignity of every person as a child of God, establishes a basic fraternity, teaches people how to encounter nature and understand work, and provides reasons for joy and humor even in the midst of a very hard life (Puebla, 448).

The tensions that Puebla mentions—divine and human, spirit and body, communion and institution, person and community, faith and homeland, intelligence and emotion—are universal. The vital synthesis, the creative bringing together of these tensions, which is indefinable in words, because that would require them all, this symbolic, living core—that for our people is translated into "proper names" such as Guadalupe and Luján, into pilgrim faith, into gestures of blessing and solidarity, into offerings, into song and dancing—this heart and the graces which our people love and believe are the theological place where the preacher has to be vitally situated. That is to say, the challenge of an inculturated preaching is to evangelize the synthesis, not free-floating ideas and values. Where your synthesis is, if I may paraphrase, there also is your heart. The difference between illuminating the site of synthesis and illuminating free-floating ideas is the same as between boredom and fervor in the heart.

It is not easy to speak about heart to the people of God. It is not enough to be well intentioned. The people appreciate and value a preacher who tries to be sincere and speaks simply in real images. But to speak of the heart means not only having one that is ardent; it must also be enlightened by the integrity of revelation, by the Word and by the path it has traveled in the heart of the Church, and of our faithful people throughout history (Tradition).

By revaluing the positive elements of popular piety, Puebla, in a rich and inspired text (454), provides a synthesis outline that is more than a mere enumeration. In each "element" collected from the heart of many pastors, there is already a synthesis. They are concrete, universal "elements" in which the totality of the faith shines embodied in typical features of the religiosity of our Latin American people. While reading from the Puebla document, I will offer a few brief suggestions that could inspire our homilies to be nourished by the synthesis and to nourish it in the hearts of listeners.

Puebla identifies a number of items as positive elements in the people's piety:

"The trinitarian presence evident
in devotions and iconography"

Our people experience the triune God as the baptismal and baptizing God, a God in whom one is plunged as an infant and in whom we live, move, and exist. The mystery of the Trinity is the life-giving environment surrounding the faith of our people rather than a specific target for rational discourse. More than our words, what should be trinitarian in our homilies are our gestures, our images, the length of time we devote to each divine person.

"A sense of God the Father's providence"

Here I would say that illuminating and nourishing the image of the Father as provident means preaching joyfully. Our people relax and enjoy it when we speak of the God who is always great, who cared for our parents and grandparents, who guides our children's future.

If our homilies are to be faithful and fruitful, they should always plant and harvest hope.

"Christ celebrated in the mystery of his Incarnation (the Nativity, the child Jesus), in his crucifixion, in the Eucharist, and in the devotion to the Sacred Heart"

Jesus is in the heart of our people as the Infant in the manger, as the dead man on the cross, as the bread of children's First Communion, and as the God with a loving heart. Sometimes noting (in a quantitative mentality) that we lack an image of the Risen One, we think that a second evangelization needs to "add" another image, or even better, to replace all the existing ones with a single image that is purer and more complete. Beyond all pretentious apologetics, it is better to start with the conviction that if the faith bore fruit, it is because it was planted whole, and to look at the images that are already in the heart, what they themselves tell us about how the heart integrates, purifies, and completes the new. The crosses arrayed in glory continue speaking to the heart of our people more than the "stop suffering" of the sects.*

"Love of Mary . . . She and 'her mysteries are part of the very identity of these peoples and characterize their popular piety' (John Paul II, Homily in Zapopan, January 30, 1979). She is venerated as the Immaculate Mother of God and of human beings, and as Queen of our individual countries as well as of the whole continent."

Puebla puts the love of Mary in the center of the passage. Mary and her mysteries "are part of the very identity of these peoples," says the Pope. In her, our people move, in a real way, with a

---

* Translator's note: the Christian Community of the Holy Spirit is a religious sect operating in Latin America, and known by its slogan "Stop Suffering."

Latin American realism that, more than magic, is a realism "full of grace," everything that a rational discourse misses regarding the presence of notions about resurrection and the Holy Spirit. Our people embody all that is positive, festive, life-giving, beautiful, joyous, and celebratory in Mary. In homilies for our people, Mary cannot be just a conclusion but, more explicitly, a central reference.

Central because she is for our people "the model of how to believe":

> *Mary, who by the eternal will of the Most High stands, one may say, at the very center of those "inscrutable ways" and "unsearchable judgments" of God, conforms herself to them in the dim light of faith, accepting fully and with a ready heart everything that is decreed in the divine plan (Redemptoris mater, 14).*

Central because she is for our people "a sign of sure hope":

> *Mary, Mother of the Incarnate Word, is placed at the very center of that enmity, that struggle which accompanies the history of humanity on earth and the history of salvation itself. In this central place, she who belongs to the "weak and poor of the Lord" bears in herself, like no other member of the human race, that "glory of grace" which the Father "has bestowed on us in his beloved Son," and this grace determines the extraordinary greatness and beauty of her whole being. Mary thus remains before God, and also before the whole of humanity, as the unchangeable and inviolable sign of God's election, spoken of in Paul's letter: "in Christ . . . he chose us . . . before the foundation of the world, . . . he destined us . . . to be his sons" (Ephesians 1:4, 5). This election is more powerful than any experience of evil and sin, than all that*

*"enmity" which marks the history of man. In this history
Mary remains a sign of sure hope (Redemptoris mater, 11).*

Central because she is for our people the locus of mercy:

*Mary is the first to share in this new revelation of God and,
within the same, in this new "self-giving" of God. Therefore
she proclaims: "For he who is mighty has done great things
for me, and holy is his name." Her words reflect a joy of spirit
which is difficult to express: "My spirit rejoices in God my
Savior." Indeed, "the deepest truth about God and the salvation of man is made clear to us in Christ, who is at the
same time the mediator and the fullness of all revelation."
In her exultation Mary confesses that she finds herself in the
very heart of this fullness of Christ. She is conscious that the
promise made to the fathers, first of all "to Abraham and
to his posterity forever," is being fulfilled in herself. She is
thus aware that concentrated within herself as the mother
of Christ is the whole salvific economy, in which "from age
to age" is manifested he who as the God of the Covenant
"remembers his mercy" (Redemptoris mater, 36).*

Of all the other elements that we have to meditate on as valuable syntheses—each of them—and to take into account when
preaching, let us highlight just one more:

*"The ability to express the faith in a total idiom that goes
beyond all sorts of rationalism (chant, images, gesture, color
and dance); faith situated in time (feasts) and in various
places (sanctuaries and shrines)."*

This faith that our faithful people express in a grounded
and complete way—complete not only in content but existen-
tially—should be echoed in the homily. The challenge consists

in reinterpreting our people's lived faith into their own language and mode of expression so that it grows and is purified from within.

As Puebla prophetically says later:

If the Church does not reinterpret the religion of the Latin American people, the resultant vacuum will be occupied by sects, secularized political forms of messianism, consumerism and its consequences of nausea and indifference, or pagan pansexualism. Once again the Church is faced with stark alternatives: what it does not assume in Christ is not redeemed, and it becomes a new idol replete with all the old malicious cunning (Puebla, 469).

The challenge still before us is a new evangelization that, as Puebla says, "has to appeal to the Christian memory of our people." The deposit of faith inculcated by mothers in the hearts of their children throughout the centuries is the living source of our identity—identity that cannot change for the better until Christ is formed in us; this identity that is the baptismal embrace that the Father gave us as little children, that made us crave, like prodigal children—and Mary's beloved children— another embrace, from the merciful Father who awaits us. Making our people feel that they are in the midst of these two embraces is the hard but beautiful task of the preacher of the Gospel.

God Cares for Our Fragility

TODAY'S READINGS speak to us of hope, the hope with which God cares for our fragility.

Isaiah expresses the hope of the people in the wish that the Messiah will come to look after the fragility of the poor, discouraged by so much bad news, wounded more in their hearts than in their bodies, living like prisoners of the interests of the powerful. And he announces that when the Anointed One comes, he will transform the desolate people into a priestly people, consoling them with the good news that he will make them proclaimers of good tidings to all other peoples. Binding their wounded hearts and freeing them from all bondage, he will make them ministers of reconciliation and freedom. Changing their garments of mourning for the oil of gladness will make all nations recognize them as a race the Lord has blessed.

Jesus, in the Gospel of Saint Luke, concentrates on himself and makes this hope his own. He turns it into a present event. He is the constant source of this priestly grace, always available to the person who is moved to entrust his fragility to Jesus' hands, to the person who believes that in the "today" of Jesus the scriptures, and all human longing, have been fulfilled. Thus, today, as priests, we want to put into the hands of the Lord, as a holy offering, our own fragility, the fragility of our people, the fragility of humanity as a whole—its discouragement, its wounds, its grief—so that offered through him it is transformed into Eucharist, the food that strengthens our hope and makes our love active in faith.

Every offering and every dialogue between God and human beings have in the Priest, Jesus, this simple, joyous character of a beautiful Eucharist, which, in the tenderness of bread, links worship with life. What does it mean for us as priests and priestly people that Jesus is Priest forever, mediator between God and human beings? It means the humble, joyful tone of one who does not want glory for himself but that his glory is to mediate, so that the good of the people will be for the glory of the Father. It means that we who participate in this priesthood must take joy in being the most humble and humbled servant of this mediation that is accomplished in Jesus. It means that the entire Church must be so humble and peaceful, so tender and united, that as a single priestly people she can be the place of mediation between God and those who do not even know about this grace and experiment with the most varied mediations. Thus, I invite you, dear brothers in the one priesthood of Jesus our Lord, that together we ask for the grace, for each other and for the entire Church, to understand the richness of the hope to which we have been called: to be mediators with Jesus and in Jesus between God and human beings. Mediators who offer, together with that of all the people of God, their own fragility.

May we humble ourselves in such a way that it becomes easy for our God and our brothers and sisters to communicate with one another through us. May our Heavenly Father feel, as he feels about the beloved Son, that through us, he can reach the least of his children with his blessing and his word. May people feel, as they feel about Jesus and the Virgin, that through us they can offer to the Lord their daily sacrifices, those that weave together their work and family life, and tell God that they love him, that they need him, and that they worship and praise him from the heart. I ask you that we take care of our priesthood by caring for this offering.

We know that unity is preserved by taking care of these mediations. And hope is the mediator par excellence when it is attentive to the small details in which the mysterious exchange of fragility for mercy is found. When there are good mediators, those who look after the details, unity is not broken. Jesus was very careful about details.

The "small detail" of the sheep that was missing.

The "small detail" of the wine that was running out.

The "small detail" of the widow who offered her two coins.

The "small detail" of not forgiving a small debt after being forgiven a large debt.

The "small detail" of having spare oil in the lamps in case the bridegroom is delayed.

The "small detail" of noticing how many loaves they had.

The "small detail" of having a small fire prepared and a fish on the grill as he was waiting for the disciples to return in the early hours of the morning.

The "small detail" of asking Peter, when so many important things were happening, if he truly loved him as a friend.

The "small detail" of not refusing to heal wounds.

They are Jesus' priestly ways to take care of

- the hope that brings us together in unity,
- the hope that no one is missing,
- the hope that joy never runs out but is superabundant and new,
- the hope that God is highly pleased with our most hidden gestures of love,
- the hope that forgiveness is contagious,

- the hope that looking after one's own little light will light up the big celebration,
- the hope that the bread is enough for everyone,
- the hope that he is always on the other shore,
- the hope that, in the end, what matters most to God is that we are his friends,
- the hope that so much pain is not left in oblivion but that, arriving in Heaven, God may kiss our wounds one by one and they may be the mark of a humble, grateful glory.

We ask the Virgin, mother of priests, mother of a priestly people, to take care of the fragility of the hope within us, her children, reminding us of what was proclaimed to us through her: nothing is impossible for God.

Bearing Witness to the End

Stephen, full of grace and power, did great wonders and signs among the people. Then some of those who belonged to the synagogue of the Freedmen (as it was called), Cyrenians, Alexandrians, and others of those from Cilicia and Asia, stood up and argued with Stephen. But they could not withstand the wisdom and the Spirit with which he spoke. Then they secretly instigated some men to say, "We have heard him speak blasphemous words against Moses and God." They stirred up the people as well as the elders and the scribes; then they suddenly confronted him, seized him, and brought him before the council. They set up false witnesses who said, "This man never stops saying things against this holy place and the law; for we have heard him say that this Jesus of Nazareth will destroy this place and will change the customs that Moses handed on to us." And all who sat in the council looked intently at him, and they saw that his face was like the face of an angel (Acts 6:8–15).

SAINT LUKE DESCRIBES the murder of Stephen, who was following in the footsteps of Jesus. His intention is to point out, in this first martyr, the way of the believer. "A disciple is not above the teacher" (Matthew 10:24), Jesus had said; the way of the disciple is the way of his Lord; a discipleship that does not conform to the most faithful following is unthinkable.

The martyrdom dimension of Christian existence is rooted in this reality, this "giving testimony," as the Lord said, and being ready to face the consequences that fidelity to the call demands.

The apostles deserted the Teacher (Matthew 26:56); Peter denied him out of fear (Matthew 26:69–75) . . . they had not yet been confirmed by the Resurrection and the power of the Holy Spirit. In Stephen, however, we see the mature disciple, shaped by this confirmation; in him the Word of God shows us the finished profile of the disciple who bears witness, of the disciple who, "full of grace and power, did great wonders and signs among the people" (Acts 6:8). Stephen was not an itinerant "miracle worker." Strength came from grace, the power of the Holy Spirit; and this was disturbing.

The scene is framed by a dispute. The members of the synagogue of the Freedmen who "stood up and argued with Stephen" (Acts 6:9) bring to mind Jesus' many discussions with Pharisees, Sadducees, Essenes, and Zealots, human alternatives to the radicalism of the Kingdom. However, the cogency of the Chosen People's history and the force of the Beatitudes were brought to bear on all their arguments and casuistry. It was the clash between the Truth and erudite sophistry, that nominalist balancing act to accept a formulation of truth denying its actual occurrence in life. These sophists "could not withstand the wisdom and the Spirit with which he spoke" (Acts 6:10). So they turned to various forms of violence: the bribe (Acts 6:11), like that of the Pharisees with the soldiers who witnessed to the Resurrection (Matthew 28:11–15), and like the Sanhedrin with Jesus himself . . . the bribe to stir up "the people as well as the elders and the scribes" (Acts 6:12), as they did with Jesus (Matthew 27:20); and, as they did with Jesus, they suddenly confronted him, seized him, and brought him before the

Sanhedrin (Matthew 27:20), and they presented false witness against him (see Matthew 26:59–61). The same methods, the same road leading to death. One final detail: at the moment of his sacrifice Stephen will utter the Teacher's words of forgiveness (Acts 7:59–60) and show signs of his triumphal entry into eternal life: "And all who sat in the council looked intently at him, and they saw that his face was like the face of an angel" (Acts 6:15; 7:55–56).

Thus ended the life of the Church's first disciple–martyr, who indicated for us the path to follow: the path of bearing witness to the end. Throughout the centuries Christian discipleship shines with countless men and women who refused to hide the faith they safeguarded in their hearts. The Holy Spirit told them what to say when brought to trial (see Mark 13:11), and they went valiantly and were transfigured in martyrdom: the strong Polycarp who stood firm at the stake without being nailed to it and whose body was transfigured, in the midst of the fire. . . . Felicity, fearless with her children. Agatha, who "content and happy, went to the jail, like a guest to a wedding, and commended her struggle to the Lord." The twenty-six Japanese on the hill of Nagasaki, praying, singing psalms, keeping up one another's spirits. The serenity of Maximilian Kolbe in taking the place of the other; the self-surrender in the Lord of Edith Stein, as she said over and over: "I don't know what God is ready to do with me, but I don't have to worry about that." And so many more, even in recent times. All follow Stephen's testimonial path and imitate his martyrdom with his face transformed to look like the face of an angel. Their hearts had assumed the Beatitude of the Lord: "Blessed are you when people hate you, and when they exclude you, revile you, and defame you on account of the Son of Man" (Luke 6:22). Men and women unashamed of Jesus Christ, who, imitating him on the cross, carried forward the life of the Church.

The Church was, is, and will be persecuted. The Lord has already warned us about it (see Matthew 24:4–14; Mark 13:9–13; Luke 21:12–19) so that we can be prepared. It will not be persecuted in its mediocre children, who compromise with the world, as did those renegades that the Book of Maccabees speaks about (see 1 Maccabees 1:11–15); these people are never persecuted. But there will be persecution of her other children, the ones who, in the midst of the cloud of witnesses, opt to keep their eyes fixed on Jesus (see Hebrews 12:1–2) and follow his step whatever the price. The Church will be persecuted to the degree that she remains faithful to the Gospel. The witness of this faithfulness disturbs the world, infuriates it, and they grind their teeth (Acts 7:54). It kills and destroys people like Stephen. Persecution is a time for the Church's faithfulness. Sometimes the persecution is frontal and direct; at other times, it is necessary to know how to recognize it within the cultural wrappings in which it comes in every epoch, hidden in mundane "rationality" of some self-styled "common sense" about normalcy and civility. The forms are many and varied, but what always provokes persecution is the foolishness of the Gospel, the scandal of the cross of Christ, the leaven of the Beatitudes. As in the cases of Jesus, Stephen, and that "great cloud of witnesses," the methods are always the same: disinformation, defamation, slander . . . to convince, to start, and, like every work of the Devil, to ensure that the persecution grows, spreads, and is justified (made to appear reasonable and not exactly persecution).

However, the temptation for the Church was and will be the same: evading the cross (see Matthew 16:22), negotiating the truth, mitigating the redemptive power of the cross of Christ to avoid persecution. Impoverished is the lukewarm Church that shuns and avoids the cross! It will not be fruitful; it will be politely socializing in sterility on the edges of acceptable culture. This is the price that the people of God pay for being ashamed of the Gospel, for giving in to the fear of witnessing.

We ask the disciple of the Lord, our first brother who testified to Jesus Christ and the Gospel, to grant us the grace never to be ashamed of the cross of Christ, never to give in to the temptation, out of fear, convenience, or comfort, to negotiate the strategy of the Kingdom, which entails poverty, humiliation, and humility; and to ask for the grace to remember every day the words of Saint Paul: "Do not be ashamed, then, of the testimony about our Lord or of me his prisoner, but join with me in suffering for the Gospel, relying on the power of God" (2 Timothy 1:8).

Guidelines for Pastoral Renewal

Introduction

I THANK THE LORD for this opportunity to speak with you, my brother bishops, the leadership of CELAM for the four-year period from 2011 to 2015. For fifty-seven years CELAM has served the twenty-two Episcopal Conferences of Latin America and the Caribbean, working in a spirit of solidarity and subsidiarity to promote, encourage, and improve collegiality among the bishops and communion between the region's Churches and their pastors.

Like yourselves, I too witnessed the powerful working of the Spirit in the Fifth General Conference of the Latin American and Caribbean Episcopate in Aparecida, in May 2007, which continues to inspire the efforts of CELAM for the desired renewal of the Particular Churches. In many of them, this renewal is clearly taking place. I would like to focus this conversation on the legacy of that fraternal encounter, which all of us have chosen to call a Continental Mission.

Characteristics of Aparecida

There are four hallmarks of the Fifth Conference. They are like four pillars for the implementation of Aparecida, and they are what make it distinctive.

1. *Starting without a Document*

Medellín, Puebla, and Santo Domingo began their work with a process of preparation that culminated in a sort of *Instrumentum laboris,* which then served as a basis for discussion, reflection, and the approval of the final document. Aparecida, on the other hand, encouraged the participation of the Particular Churches in a process of preparation culminating in a document of synthesis. This document, while serving as a point of reference throughout the Fifth General Conference, was not taken as a starting point. The initial work consisted in pooling the concerns expressed by the bishops as they considered the new period of history in which we are living and the need to renew the life of discipleship and mission with which Christ founded the Church.

2. *A Setting of Prayer with the People of God*

It is important to remember the prayerful setting created by the daily sharing of the Eucharist and other liturgical moments, in which we were always accompanied by the People of God. On the other hand, since the deliberations took place in the crypt of the shrine, the music that accompanied them were the songs and the prayers of the faithful.

3. *A Document That Continues in Commitment with the Continental Mission*

This context of prayer and the life of faith gave rise to a desire for a new Pentecost for the Church and the commitment to undertake a Continental Mission. Aparecida did not end with a document; it continues in the Continental Mission.

4. *The Presence of Our Lady, Mother of America*

It was the first conference of the bishops of Latin America and the Caribbean to be held in a Marian shrine.

Dimensions of the Continental Mission

The Continental Mission is planned along two lines: the programmatic and the paradigmatic. The programmatic mission, as its name indicates, consists in a series of missionary activities. The paradigmatic mission, on the other hand, involves setting in a missionary key all the day-to-day activities of the Particular Churches. Clearly this entails a whole process of reforming ecclesial structures. The "change of structures" (from obsolete ones to new ones) will not be the result of reviewing an organizational flow chart, which would lead to a static reorganization; rather it will result from the very dynamics of mission. What makes obsolete structures pass away, what leads to a change of heart in Christians, is precisely *missionary spirit*. Hence the importance of the paradigmatic mission.

The Continental Mission, both programmatic and paradigmatic, calls for creating a sense of a Church that is organized to serve all the baptized, men and women of goodwill. Christ's followers are not individuals caught up in a privatized spirituality, but persons in community, devoting themselves to others. The Continental Mission thus implies *membership in the Church*.

An approach like this, which begins with missionary discipleship and involves understanding Christian identity as membership in the Church, demands that we clearly articulate *the real challenges* facing missionary discipleship. Here I will mention only two: the Church's inner renewal and dialogue with the world around us.

The Church's Inner Renewal
Aparecida considered pastoral conversion to be a necessity. This conversion involves believing in the Good News, believing in Jesus Christ as the bearer of God's Kingdom as it breaks

into the world and in his victorious presence over evil, believing in the help and guidance of the Holy Spirit, believing in the Church, the Body of Christ, and in the prolonging of the dynamism of the Incarnation.

Consequently, we, as pastors, need to ask questions about the actual state of the churches that we lead. These questions can serve as a guide in examining where the dioceses stand in taking up the spirit of Aparecida; they are questions that we need to keep asking as an examination of conscience.

1. Do we see to it that our work, and that of our priests, is more pastoral than administrative? Who primarily benefits from our efforts, the Church as an organization or the People of God as a whole?

2. Do we fight the temptation simply to react to complex problems as they arise? Are we creating a proactive mindset? Do we promote opportunities and possibilities to manifest God's mercy? Are we conscious of our responsibility for refocusing pastoral approaches and the functioning of Church structures for the benefit of the faithful and society?

3. In practice, do we make the lay faithful sharers in the mission? Do we offer them the Word of God and the sacraments with a clear awareness and conviction that the Holy Spirit makes himself manifest in them?

4. Is pastoral discernment a habitual criterion, through the use of diocesan councils? Do such councils and parish councils, whether pastoral or financial, provide real opportunities for lay people to participate in pastoral consultation, organization, and planning? The good functioning of these councils is critical. I believe that on this score, we are far behind.

5. As pastors, bishops, and priests, are we conscious and convinced of the mission of the lay faithful and do we give them the freedom to continue discerning, in a way befitting their growth

as disciples, the mission that the Lord has entrusted to them? Do we support them and accompany them, overcoming the temptation to manipulate them or infantilize them? Are we constantly open to letting ourselves be challenged in our efforts to advance the good of the Church and her mission in the world?

6. Do pastoral agents and the faithful in general feel part of the Church? Do they identify with her and bring her closer to the baptized who are distant and alienated?

As can be appreciated, what is at stake here are *attitudes*. Pastoral conversion is chiefly concerned with attitudes and reforming our lives. A change of attitudes is necessarily something ongoing: "it is a process," and it can only be kept on track with the help of guidance and discernment. It is important always to keep in mind that the compass preventing us from going astray is that of Catholic identity, understood as membership in the Church.

Dialogue with the World around Us

We do well to recall the words of the Second Vatican Council: "The joys and hopes, the grief and anguish of the people of our time, especially of those who are poor or afflicted, are the joys and hopes, the grief and anguish of the followers of Christ as well" (*Gaudium et spes*, 1). Here we find the basis for our dialogue with the contemporary world.

Responding to the existential issues of people today, especially the young, listening to the language they speak, can lead to a fruitful change, which must take place with the help of the Gospel, the magisterium, and the Church's social doctrine. The scenarios and the institutions involved are quite varied. For example, a single city can contain various collective imaginations that create "different cities." If we remain within the parameters of our "traditional culture," which was essentially rural, we will end up nullifying the power of the Holy Spirit. God is everywhere: we have to know how to find him in order to be able to proclaim him in the language of each and every culture; every reality, every language, has its own rhythm.

Some Temptations against Missionary Discipleship

The decision for missionary discipleship will encounter temptation. It is important to know where the evil spirit is afoot in order to aid our discernment. It is not a matter of chasing after demons, but simply one of clear-sightedness and evangelical astuteness. I will mention only a few attitudes that are evidence of a Church that is "tempted." It has to do with recognizing certain contemporary proposals that can parody the process of missionary discipleship and hold back, even bring to a halt, the process of pastoral conversion.

1. *Making the Gospel message an ideology.* This is a temptation that has been present in the Church from the beginning: the attempt to interpret the Gospel apart from the Gospel itself and apart from the Church. An example: Aparecida, at one particular moment, felt this temptation. It employed, and rightly so, the method of "see, judge, and act" (see No. 19). The temptation, though, was to opt for a way of "seeing" that was completely "antiseptic," detached, and unengaged, which is impossible. The way we "see" is always affected by the way we direct our gaze. There is no such thing as an "antiseptic" hermeneutics. The question was, rather: How are we going to look at reality in order to see it? Aparecida replied, With the eyes of discipleship. This is the way Nos. 20–32 are to be understood. There are other ways of making the message an ideology, and at present, proposals of this sort are appearing in Latin America and the Caribbean. I mention only a few:

(a) Sociological reductionism. This is the most readily available means of making the message an ideology. At certain times it has proved extremely influential. It involves an interpretative claim based on a hermeneutics drawn from the social sciences. It extends to the most varied fields, from market liberalism to Marxist categorization.

(b) Psychologizing. Here we have to do with an elitist hermeneutics that ultimately reduces the "encounter with Jesus Christ" and its development to a process of growing self-awareness. It is ordinarily to be found in spirituality courses, spiritual retreats, and the like. It ends up being an immanent, self-centered approach. It has nothing to do with transcendence and, consequently, with missionary spirit.

(c) The gnostic solution. Closely linked to the previous temptation, it is ordinarily found in elite groups offering a higher spirituality, generally disembodied, which ends up in a preoccupation with certain pastoral *quaestiones disputatae*. It was the first deviation in the early community, and it reappears throughout the Church's history in ever-new and revised versions. Generally its adherents are known as "enlightened Catholics" (since they are in fact rooted in the culture of the Enlightenment).

(d) The Pelagian solution. This basically appears as a form of restorationism. In dealing with the Church's problems, a purely disciplinary solution is sought through the restoration of outdated manners and forms that, even on the cultural level, are no longer meaningful. In Latin America it is usually to be found in small groups, in some new religious congregations, in exaggerated tendencies toward doctrinal or disciplinary "safety." Basically it is static, although it is capable of inversion, in a process of regression. It seeks to "recover" the lost past.

2. *Functionalism*. Its effect on the Church is paralyzing. More than being interested in the road itself, it is concerned with fixing holes in the road. A functionalist approach has no room for mystery; it aims at efficiency. It reduces the reality of the Church to the structure of an NGO. What counts are quantifiable results and statistics. The Church ends up being run like any other business organization. It applies a sort of "theology of prosperity" to the organization of pastoral work.

3. *Clericalism* is also a temptation very present in Latin America. Curiously, in the majority of cases, it has to do with a sinful complicity: the priest clericalizes the lay person and the lay person kindly asks to be clericalized, because deep down it is easier. The phenomenon of clericalism explains, in great part, the lack of maturity and Christian freedom in some of the Latin American laity. Either they simply do not grow (the majority), or else they take refuge in forms of ideology such as those we have just seen, or in partial and limited ways of belonging. Yet in our countries there does exist a form of freedom of the laity that finds expression in communal experiences: Catholic as community. Here one sees a greater autonomy, which on the whole is a healthy thing, basically expressed through popular piety. The chapter of the Aparecida document on popular piety describes this dimension in detail. The spread of Bible study groups, of ecclesial basic communities, and of pastoral councils is in fact helping to overcome clericalism and to increase lay responsibility.

We could continue by describing other temptations against missionary discipleship, but I consider these to be the most important and influential at present.

Some Ecclesiological Guidelines

1. The missionary discipleship that Aparecida proposed to the Churches of Latin America and the Caribbean is the

journey that God desires for the present "today." Every utopian (future-oriented) or restorationist (past-oriented) impulse is spiritually unhealthy. God is real, and he shows himself in the "today." With regard to the past, his presence is given to us as "memory" of his saving work, both in his people and in each of us as individuals; with regard to the future, he gives himself to us as "promise" and hope. In the past God was present and left his mark: memory helps us to encounter him; in the future is promise alone . . . he is not in the thousand-and-one things that might happen in the future. The "today" is closest to eternity; even more: the "today" is a flash of eternity. In the "today," eternal life is in play.

Missionary discipleship is a vocation: a call and an invitation. It is given in the "today" but also "in tension." There is no such thing as static missionary discipleship. A missionary disciple cannot be his own master; his immanence is in tension toward the transcendence of discipleship and the transcendence of mission. It does not allow for self-absorption: either it points to Jesus Christ or it points to the people to whom he must be proclaimed. The missionary disciple is a self-transcending subject, a subject projected toward encounter: an encounter with the Master (who anoints us as his disciples) and an encounter with men and women who await the message.

That is why I like saying that the position of missionary disciples is not in the center but at the periphery: they live poised toward the peripheries . . . including the peripheries of eternity, in the encounter with Jesus Christ. In the preaching of the Gospel, to speak of "existential peripheries" decentralizes things; as a rule, we are afraid to leave the center. The missionary disciple is someone "off-center": the center is Jesus Christ, who calls us and sends us forth. The disciple is sent to the existential peripheries.

2. The Church is an institution, but when she makes herself a "center," she becomes merely functional and slowly but surely turns into a kind of NGO. The Church then claims to have a light of her own, and she stops being that *mysterium lunae* of which the Church Fathers spoke. She becomes increasingly self-referential and loses her need to be missionary. From an "institution" she becomes an "enterprise." She stops being a bride and ends up being an administrator; from being a servant, she becomes an "inspector." Aparecida wanted a Church that is bride, mother, and servant, more a facilitator of faith than an inspector of faith.

3. In Aparecida, two pastoral categories stand out; they arise from the uniqueness of the Gospel, and we can employ them as guidelines for assessing how we are living missionary discipleship in the Church: *nearness* and *encounter*. Neither of these two categories is new; rather, they are the way God has revealed himself to us in history. He is the "God who is near" to his people, a nearness that culminates in the Incarnation. He is the God who goes forth to meet his people. In Latin America and the Caribbean there are pastoral plans that are "distant," disciplinary pastoral plans that give priority to principles, forms of conduct, organizational procedures . . . and clearly lack nearness, tenderness, a warm touch. They do not take into account the "revolution of tenderness" brought by the Incarnation of the Word. There are pastoral plans designed with such a dose of distance that they are incapable of sparking an encounter: an encounter with Jesus Christ, an encounter with our brothers and sisters. Such pastoral plans can at best provide a dimension of proselytism, but they can never inspire people to feel part of or belong to the Church. Nearness creates communion and belonging; it makes room for encounter. Nearness takes the form of dialogue and creates a culture of encounter. One

touchstone for measuring whether a pastoral plan embodies nearness and a capacity for encounter is the homily. What are our homilies like? Do we imitate the example of our Lord, who spoke "as one with authority," or are they simply moralizing, detached, abstract?

4. Those who direct pastoral work, the Continental Mission (both programmatic and paradigmatic), are the bishops. Bishops must lead, which is not the same thing as being authoritarian. As well as pointing to the great figures of the Latin American episcopate, whom we all know, I would like to add a few things about the profile of the bishop, which I already presented to the Nuncios at our meeting in Rome. Bishops must be pastors, close to people, fathers and brothers, and gentle, patient, and merciful. Men who love poverty, both interior poverty, as freedom before the Lord, and exterior poverty, as simplicity and austerity of life. Men who do not think and behave like "princes." Men who are not ambitious, who are married to one church without having their eyes on another. Men capable of watching over the flock entrusted to them and protecting everything that keeps it together: guarding their people out of concern for the dangers that could threaten them, but above all instilling hope: so that light will shine in people's hearts. Men capable of supporting with love and patience God's dealings with his people. The bishop has to be among his people in three ways: in front of them, pointing the way; among them, keeping them together and preventing them from being scattered; and behind them, ensuring that no one is left behind, but also, and primarily, so that the flock itself can sniff out new paths.

I do not wish to go into further detail about the person of the bishop, but simply to add, including myself in this statement, that we are lagging somewhat as far as pastoral conversion is concerned. We need to help one another a bit more in taking the steps that the Lord asks of us in the "today" of Latin America and the Caribbean. And this is a good place to start.

I thank you for your patience in listening to me. Pardon me if my remarks have been somewhat disjointed, and please, I beg that we take seriously our calling as servants of the holy and faithful people of God, for this is where authority is exercised and demonstrated: in the ability to serve. Many thanks.

Three Basic Qualities of Becoming Church

THANK YOU for your welcome, priests, men and women religious, laity engaged in pastoral councils! How needed pastoral councils are! A bishop cannot guide a diocese without pastoral councils. A parish priest cannot guide the parish without the parish council. This is fundamental! We are in the cathedral! Here is the baptismal font where Sts. Francis and Clare were baptized; in their day it was located in the Church of Santa Maria. The memory of one's Baptism is important! Baptism is our birth as children of Holy Mother Church. I would like to ask you a question: Who among you knows the day you were baptized? So few, so few . . . now, here is your homework! Mother, Father, tell me: when was I baptized? It's very important, because it was the day of your birth as a child of God. One Spirit, one Baptism, in a variety of charisms and ministries. What a great gift it is to be the Church, to be a part of the People of God! Together we are the People of God—in harmony, in the communion of gift of harmony in diversity which is the work of the Holy Spirit, because the Holy Spirit is harmony and creates harmony: it is his gift, and we should be open to receive it.

The bishop is the guardian of this harmony. The bishop is the guardian of this diversity. That is why Pope Benedict wished that the pastoral activity in the Franciscan papal basilicas be integrated into the diocesan one. For he has to create harmony:

it is his task, his duty, and his vocation. I am glad that you are advancing nicely on this road, and to the benefit of all, by peacefully working together. I encourage you to continue in this. The pastoral visit that has just ended and the diocesan synod that you are about to celebrate are intense moments of growth for this Church that God has blessed in a special way. The Church grows, but not through proselytizing: no, no! The Church does not grow through proselytizing. The Church grows through attraction, through the attraction of the witness that each one of us gives to the People of God.

Now, briefly, I would like to highlight several aspects of your life as a community. I do not wish to tell you something new, but rather to confirm you in those things that are most important, and that mark your journey as a diocese.

1. The first thing is *to listen to God's Word*. This is what the Church is: it is the community that listens with faith and love to the Lord who speaks. The pastoral plan that you are living out together insists precisely on this fundamental dimension. It is the Word of God that inspires faith, which nourishes and revitalizes it. And it is the Word of God that touches hearts, converts them to God and to his logic, which is so different from our own. It is the Word of God that continually renews our communities.

I think we can all improve a bit in this respect: by becoming better listeners of the Word of God, in order to be less rich in our own words and richer in his words. I think of the priest who has the task of preaching. How can he preach if he has not first opened his heart, not listened in silence to the Word of God? Away with these never-ending, boring homilies that no one understands. This is for you! I think of fathers and mothers, who are the primary educators [of their children]: how can they educate them if their consciences have not been enlightened by the Word of God. If their way of thinking and acting is not guided by the Word, what sort of example can they possibly give to their children? This is important, because then mothers and fathers complain: "Oh, this child . . ." But you, what witness have you given the child? How have you spoken to him? Have you talked with him about the Word of God or about TV news? Fathers and mothers need to be talking about the Word of God! And I think of catechists and of all those who are involved in education. If their hearts have not been warmed by the Word, how can they warm the hearts of others, of children, of youth, of adults? It is not enough just to read the Sacred Scriptures, we need to listen to Jesus who speaks in them. It is Jesus himself who speaks in the Scriptures; it is Jesus who speaks in them. We need to be receiving antennas that are tuned into the Word of God, in order to become broadcasting antennas! One receives and transmits. It is the Spirit of God who makes the Scriptures come alive, who makes us understand them deeply and in accord with their authentic and full meaning! Let us ask ourselves: What place does the Word of God have in my life, in my everyday life? Am I tuned into God or into the many buzz words or into myself? This is a question that everyone of us needs to ask him- or herself.

2. The second aspect is *walking.* It is one of my favorite words when I think about a Christian and about the Church. However, it has a special meaning for you. You are about to enter into the diocesan synod. To hold a "synod" means to walk together. I think this is truly the most wonderful experience we can have: to belong to a people walking, journeying through history together with their Lord who walks among us! We are not alone, we do not walk alone. We are part of the one flock of Christ that walks together.

Here I think once more of you priests, and let me place myself in your company. What could be more beautiful for us than walking with our people? It is beautiful! I think of the parish priests who knew the names of their parishioners, who went to visit them; even as one of them told me, "I know the name of each family's dog." They even knew the dog's name! How nice it was! What could be more beautiful than this? I repeat it often: walking with our people, sometimes in front, sometimes in the middle, and sometimes behind: in front in order to guide the community; in the middle in order to encourage and support; and at the back in order to keep it united and so that no one lags too, too far behind, to keep them united. There is another reason too: because the people have a "nose"! The people scent, discover, new ways to walk; it has the *sensus fidei*, as theologians call it. What could be more beautiful than this? During the synod, it will be very important to consider what the Holy Spirit is saying to the laity, to the People of God, to everyone.

But the most important thing is to walk together by working together, by helping one another, by asking forgiveness, by acknowledging one's mistakes and asking for forgiveness, and also by accepting the apologies of others by forgiving—how important this is! Sometimes I think of married people who separate after many years. "Oh . . . no, we didn't understand each other, we drifted apart." Perhaps at times they didn't know how to ask for forgiveness at the right time. Perhaps at times they did not know how to forgive. And I always give this advice to newlyweds: "Argue as much as you like. If the plates fly, let them! But never end the day without making peace! Never!" And if married people learn to say, "Excuse me, I was tired," or even a little gesture, there is peace. Then carry on with life the next day. This is a beautiful secret, and it prevents these painful separations. It is important to walk in unity, without running ahead, without nostalgia for the past. And while you walk you talk, you get to know one another, you tell each other about yourself, you grow as a family. Here let us ask ourselves: How do we walk? How does our diocese walk? Does it walk together? And what am I doing so that it may truly walk in unity? I do not wish to enter into a discussion here about gossip, but you know that gossip always divides.

3. Therefore: listen, and walk. And the third aspect is missionary: *to proclaim even to the outskirts*. I also borrowed this from you, from your pastoral plan. The bishop spoke recently about it. However, I wish to emphasize it, because it is something I also experienced a great deal when I was in Buenos Aires: the importance of going out to meet the other in the outskirts, which are places but which are primarily people living in particular situations in life. This was true in my former diocese, that of Buenos Aires. The outskirts that hurt me a great deal was to find children in middle-class families who didn't know how to make the Sign of the Cross. But you see, this is an outskirt! And I ask you, here in this diocese, are there children who do not know how to make the Sign of the Cross? Think about it. These are true outskirts of existence, where God is absent.

In one sense, the outskirts of this diocese, for example, are the areas of the diocese that risk being left on the margins, beyond the street lights. But they are also people and human realities that are marginalized and despised. They are people who perhaps live physically close to the "center" but who spiritually are very far away.

Do not be afraid to go out and meet these people and situations. Do not allow yourselves to be impeded by prejudice, by habit, by an intellectual or pastoral rigidity, by the famous "we've always done it this way!" However, we can only go to the outskirts if we carry the Word of God in our hearts and if we walk with the Church, like St. Francis. Otherwise, we take ourselves, not the Word of God, and this isn't good; it doesn't help anyone! We are not the ones who save the world; it is the Lord himself who saves it!

There you are, dear friends. I haven't given you any new recipes. I don't have any, and don't believe anyone who says he does; they don't exist. However, I did find several beautiful and important aspects of the journey of your Church that should be developed, and I want to confirm you in these. Listen to the Word, walk together as brothers and sisters, proclaim the Gospel to the outskirts! May the Lord bless you, may Our Lady protect you, and may St. Francis help you all to experience the joy of being disciples of the Lord! Thank you.

The New Evangelization

WHAT I WOULD LIKE to tell you today may be summarized in three points: the primacy of witness; the urgency of going out to meet others; the need for a pastoral plan centered on the essential.

1. Often today there is an attitude of indifference toward the faith, an indifference that regards it as irrelevant for human life. The New Evangelization means reawakening the life of faith in the minds and hearts of our contemporaries. Faith is a gift of God; however, it is important that we Christians demonstrate that we live faith in a concrete way, through love, harmony, joy, suffering, because this gives rise to questions such as those that were raised at the beginning of the Church's journey: Why do they live that way? What urges them on? These are questions that lead straight to the heart of evangelization, to the *witness* of faith and charity. What we especially need in these times are credible witnesses who make the Gospel visible by their lives as well as by their words, and who reawaken the attraction for Jesus Christ, for the beauty of God.

Many people have drifted away from the Church. It would be a mistake to place the blame on one side or the other; indeed, there is no need even to speak of blame. The responsibility lies in the history of the Church and her people—in certain ideologies and also in individuals. As children of the Church we must continue on the journey of the Second Vatican Council and divest ourselves of useless and hurtful things, of false worldly security that weighs down the Church and injures her true face.

We need Christians who make God's mercy and tenderness for every creature visible to the people of our day. We all know that the crisis of modern man is not superficial but profound. That is why the New Evangelization, while it calls us to have the courage to swim against the tide and to be converted from idols to the true God, cannot but use a language of mercy, which is expressed in gestures and attitudes even before words. The Church says as she stands amid humanity today: Come to Jesus, all you who labor and are heavy laden, and you will find rest for your souls (Matthew 11:28–30). Come to Jesus. He alone has the words of eternal life.

Every baptized Christian is a "*Christopher,*" that is, a Christ-bearer, as the Church Fathers used to say. Whoever has encountered Christ, like the Samaritan woman at the well, cannot keep this experience to himself but feels the need to share it and to lead others to Jesus (see John 4). We all need to ask ourselves if those who encounter us perceive the warmth of faith in our lives, if they see in our faces the joy of having encountered Christ!

2. Here we pass to the second aspect: encounter, *going out to meet others.* The New Evangelization is a renewed movement toward those who have lost the faith and a sense of the deep meaning of life. This dynamism is part of Christ's great mission to bring life to the world, to bring the Father's love to humanity. The Son of God "went forth" from his divine condition and came to meet us. The Church abides within this movement; every Christian is called to go out to meet others, to dialogue with those who do not think as we do, with those who have another faith or who have no faith. To encounter all, because

what we all share in common is that we were created in the image and likeness of God. We can go out to everyone without fear and without renouncing our membership in the Church.

No one is excluded from life's hope, from God's love. The Church is sent to reawaken this hope everywhere, especially where it has been suffocated by difficult and oftentimes inhuman living conditions; where hope cannot breathe, it suffocates. We need the fresh air of the Gospel, the breath of the Spirit of the Risen Christ, to rekindle hope in people's hearts. The Church is the home where the doors are always open, not only because everyone finds a welcome and is able to breathe in love and hope, but also because we can go out bearing this love and this hope. The Holy Spirit urges us to go beyond our own narrow confines, and he guides us to the outskirts of humanity.

3. However, in the Church all of this cannot be left to chance or improvisation. It requires a shared commitment to a pastoral plan that brings us back to the essential and that is *solidly focused on the essential; that is, on Jesus Christ.* To get diverted by many secondary or superfluous things does not help; what helps is to focus on the fundamental reality, which is the encounter with Christ, with his mercy and with his love, and to love our brothers and sisters as he has loved us. An encounter with Christ is also adoration, a little-used word: to adore Christ. We need a plan animated by the creativity and imagination of the Holy Spirit, who also urges us to take new paths with courage without becoming fossils! We might ask ourselves: What is the pastoral plan of our dioceses or parishes like? Does it make the essential visible, namely, Jesus Christ? Do the various experiences and features that the Holy Spirit grants journey together in harmony? Or is our pastoral plan dissipated and fragmented, such that in the end everyone goes his own way? In this context I would like to emphasize the importance of catechesis as

a moment for evangelization. Pope Paul VI spoke of it some years ago in *Evangelii Nuntiandi* (no. 44). Starting from there, the great catechetical movement has promoted renewal to overcome the split between the Gospel and culture and the illiteracy that exists today in matters of faith. I have recalled many times something that greatly impressed me in my ministry: meeting children who did not even know how to make the Sign of the Cross! In our cities! The role that catechists play is a truly valuable service for the New Evangelization, and it is important that parents be the first catechists, the first educators of the faith in their own family by their witness and by their word.

Thank you, dear friends, for this visit. I wish you the best in your work! May the Lord bless you, and may Our Lady protect you.

Sources

Words from the Upper Room (pp. 1–3) • Homily at Mass with the ordinaries of the Holy Land and the papal entourage, on the occasion of the fiftieth anniversary of the meeting between Pope Paul VI and Patriarch Athenagoras in Jerusalem (May 26, 2014)

A Heart That Is Moved (pp. 4–12) • Address to the parish priests of the Diocese of Rome (March 6, 2014)

Do You Love Me? (pp. 13–17) • Address at the Italian Episcopal Conference (May 23, 2013)

When We Pray, We Are Fighting for Our People (pp. 18–24) • Letter to the priests and religious of the archdiocese (2007)

Shepherds with the Odor of Sheep (pp. 25–27) • Homily at the Ninety-first Plenary Assembly of Bishops (May 2006)

Do the People Leave Us Looking Like They Have Heard the Good News? (pp. 28–32) • Homily at the Chrism Mass (March 28, 2013)

The Grace of Apostolic Audacity (pp. 33–36) • Homily at the Chrism Mass (2004)

With Hearts Burning from Within (pp. 37–41) • Homily at the Chrism Mass (2001)

Evangelical Openness (pp. 42–47) • Address to the priests of the archdiocese (October 1999)

Primary Features of Priestly Joy (pp. 48–53) • Homily at the Chrism Mass (April 17, 2014)

The Oil of Gladness (pp. 54–56) • Homily at the Chrism Mass (2000)

The Importance of Anointing (pp. 57–60) • Homily at the Chrism Mass (2002)

The Perfect Gift (pp. 61–65) • Homily at the Chrism Mass (2006)

The "Today" of Jesus (pp. 66–69) • Homily at the Chrism Mass (2005)

The Grace of Unity (pp. 70–73) • Homily at the Ninety-second Plenary Assembly of Bishops (November 2006)

The Lively Dialogue That Is Preaching (pp. 74–88) • Address at the Plenary Assembly of the Commission for Latin America, Rome (January 2005)

God Cares for Our Fragility (pp. 89–92) • Homily at the Chrism Mass (2003)

Bearing Witness to the End (pp. 93–97) • Homily at the Episcopal Assembly (April 2007)

Guidelines for Pastoral Renewal (pp. 98–109) • Address to the leadership of the Episcopal Conferences of Latin America during the General Coordination Meeting (July 28, 2013)

Three Basic Qualities of Becoming Church (pp. 110–115) • Address at meeting with clergy, consecrated people, and members of diocesan pastoral councils in Cathedral of San Rufino, Assisi (October 4, 2013)

The New Evangelization (pp. 116–119) • Address to participants in the Plenary of the Pontifical Council for Promoting the New Evangelization (October 14, 2013)

About the Translator

MICHAEL O'HEARN has been involved in religious and university publishing for over thirty-five years. He served as director of both the University of Ottawa Press and of Novalis Publishing at Saint Paul University, where he was also a lecturer in pastoral theology. He currently works as a translator (Spanish and French) and editor of religious and academic resources.

About the Publisher

The CROSSROAD PUBLISHING COMPANY publishes
CROSSROAD and HERDER & HERDER books. We offer
a 200-year global family tradition of books on spiritual
living and religious thought. We promote reading as a
time-tested discipline for focus and understanding. We
help authors shape, clarify, write, and effectively promote their ideas. We select, edit, and distribute books.
With our expertise and passion we provide wholesome
spiritual nourishment for heart, mind, and soul through
the written word.

You Might Also Like

POPE FRANCIS (Jorge Mario Bergoglio)
Open Mind, Faithful Heart
Reflections on Following Jesus

Paperback, 320 pages, ISBN 978-0-8245-2085-4

"The secret of Pope Francis is found in this book."
—Bishop Martínez Camino

This is the book that Pope Francis wished for, initiated, and actively worked on just before he was elected Pope. The texts of this volume, handpicked by the author for this volume, reveal the spiritual depth of Pope Francis as perhaps no other work does. The language of these pages speaks to the heart as much as to the mind. These are meditations to be savored, and read again and again.

"Among the large number of publications that have appeared in the months since the conclave, we do well to distinguish between books 'about' the Pope, and books 'of the Pope' ... the Pope's own books, of which this is [the last before he was elected], come directly from his own hand. . . . These are the books that show us all the depth and breadth of Francis."
—Gustavo Larrazabal, CFM
The Editor of the Pope

Please support your local bookstore or order directly from the publisher at www.crossroadpublishing.com.

To request a catalog or inquire about quantity orders, please email sales@crossroadpublishing.com

The Crossroad Publishing Company